A Treasury of Trickster Tales

By Valerie Marsh

Illustrated by Patrick K. Luzadder

Alleyside Press®

Fort Atkinson, Wisconsin

To all of us who have ever:

played a practical joke,

tried to get someone else to do our work for us,

or

secretly enjoyed watching someone else pull a harmless trick.

After all... isn't there is a little bit of trickster in everyone one of us?

꙳

Published by Alleyside Press,
an imprint of Highsmith Press LLC
Highsmith Press
W5527 Highway 106
P.O. Box 800
Fort Atkinson, Wisconsin 53538-0800
1-800-558-2110

© Valerie Marsh, 1997
Cover design: Frank Neu

The paper used in this publication meets the minimum requirements of American National
Standard for Information Science — Permanence of Paper for Printed Library Material.
ANSI/NISO Z39.48-1992.

Library of Congress Cataloging-in-Publication Data
Marsh, Valerie.
    A treasury of trickster tales / by Valerie Marsh ; illustrated by
Patrick K. Luzadder.
      p. cm.
    ISBN 0-917846-91-5   (soft : alk. paper)
    1. Storytelling. 2. Trickster in literature. 3. Folklore–Study
and teaching. 4. Teaching–Aids and devices. I. Title.
LB1042.M288 1997
372.67'7–dc21   97-5208
                                                              CIP

Contents

Story Method Icons

Paper-Cutting   Mystery-Fold   Sign Language   Storyknifing   Story Puzzles

Roger the Trickster

Other Tricksters

Story Method Directions

Introduction

Trickster! That's what you would call someone who tricked you out of your lunch.

Deceiver! That's what you would call someone who got you to do their work for them. Even though different cultures have different tricksters, these tricksters often cause or get into the same kinds of trouble. Why is that? Is it because people are pretty much the same no matter where they live? Or is it because, as people move around in the world, they bring their stories with them to tell in their new homes?

Tricksters are complex and contradictory. They are clever one time, and just plain silly the next time. They set out to be good and end up being bad. They represent the chaotic, unpredictable elements of a (sometimes) well-ordered society. In all these facets, they represent life itself.

Tricksters are always trying to get away with something. Tricksters can take the form of a bird, an animal, or even a person. Many cultures have one trickster who is more important in their stories than other tricksters. If need be, they can change from one shape into another. Although their pranks occasionally can be harmful, they mostly play innocent tricks on their fellow earth creatures.

Occasionally, the trickster, in trying to trick, gets tricked himself. Then he finds himself caught in his own trap. Immediately he sets out to "weasel" his way out of it!

Oftentimes, the trickster starts out as the underdog. He is a small, defenseless, little-respected creature who must use his cunning and wits to get what he wants. This is because he is not strong enough to take it by force. At the end of the story, the harmless looking trickster has created more havoc than a larger, more powerful creature could have.

We like to see the little guy win against impossible odds. For isn't that what we as humans try to do so many times in life? We are small and defenseless against such powerful enemies as weather, hunger, natural disasters, and even the ever-present enemy of our own human nature. We must use our wits in order to survive and thrive. Because of this, we all enjoy hearing about a trickster who does just that!

In this book, you will find a variety of tricksters. The tricksters themselves contain representative elements from cultures around the world. The stories, while placed in a particular culture, have very similar motifs or themes that appear in many other cultures in a variety of renditions.

To give your storytelling added variety, these trickster tales are told in one of five storytelling methods:

Paper-cutting stories involve telling a story while cutting a piece of folded paper. At the end of the story, unfold the paper to reveal your surprise object.

Mystery-fold stories involve drawing a picture and then folding your paper together at the end of your story to make a surprise picture.

Sign language stories are told with key words in sign language so that listeners can join in the telling with you.

Story puzzles are tangram puzzle pieces that are used to make simple shapes to enhance the story.

Storyknifing is a simple drawing method used to pique the listener's interest.

Each of these storytelling methods interprets an individual story in an interesting, and often dramatic way. Directions, patterns and other helpful information on each is located in the Story Method Directions at the back of the book. You can choose your favorite storytelling method and then tell those trickster tales with that method. Or you can choose your favorite tricksters and tell their stories.

Either way—it's an easy, fun, and creative way to "trick" your audience into listening spellbound!

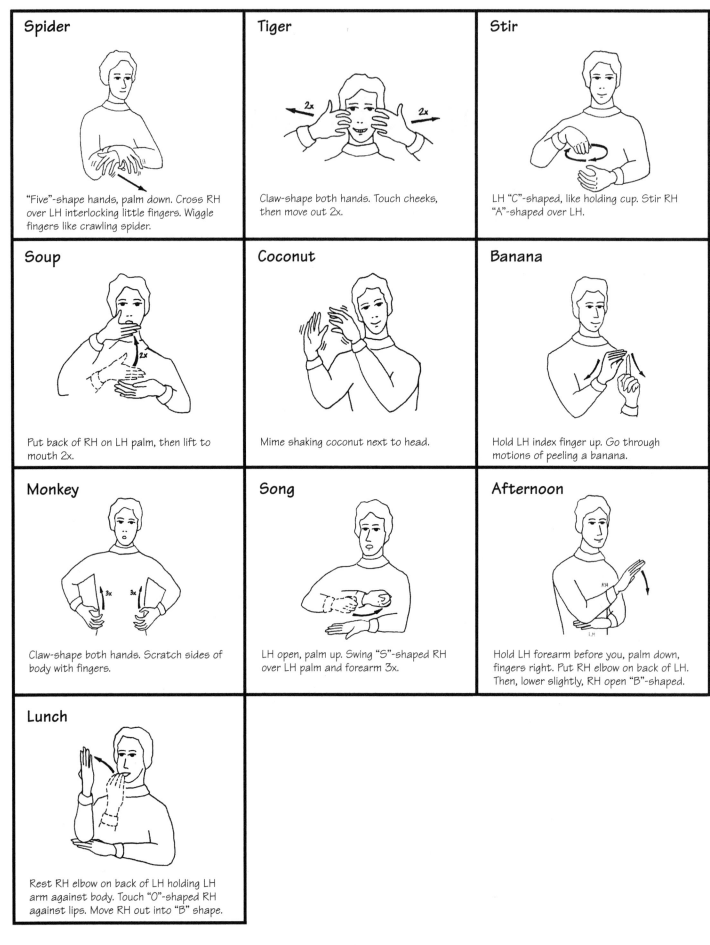

Spider
"Five"-shape hands, palm down. Cross RH over LH interlocking little fingers. Wiggle fingers like crawling spider.

Tiger
Claw-shape both hands. Touch cheeks, then move out 2x.

Stir
LH "C"-shaped, like holding cup. Stir RH "A"-shaped over LH.

Soup
Put back of RH on LH palm, then lift to mouth 2x.

Coconut
Mime shaking coconut next to head.

Banana
Hold LH index finger up. Go through motions of peeling a banana.

Monkey
Claw-shape both hands. Scratch sides of body with fingers.

Song
LH open, palm up. Swing "S"-shaped RH over LH palm and forearm 3x.

Afternoon
Hold LH forearm before you, palm down, fingers right. Put RH elbow on back of LH. Then, lower slightly, RH open "B"-shaped.

Lunch
Rest RH elbow on back of LH holding LH arm against body. Touch "O"-shaped RH against lips. Move RH out into "B" shape.

Anansi and the Tiger's Soup

Anansi and the Tiger's Soup

This is a story about how Anansi the Spider pulls a trick on one of his friends. We can use sign language to tell this story together. First, I want to share the signs that we will be using in this story.

This is the sign for **spider** which we will be using to represent Anansi the Spider. Can you do this sign with me? Good. We will also meet **Tiger** in this story. He is **stirring soup** for his **lunch**. These are the signs for **stir, soup**, and **lunch**. Can you do these signs with me? Great. Now let's begin our story.

One fine day, **Anansi the Spider** was walking through the forest when he came upon **Tiger**, who was standing over a big pot, **stirring** and **stirring**.

Anansi called to **Tiger**, "What are you **stirring** there, my fine friend?"

Tiger answered, "I'm making a **soup** for my **lunch**."

"It smells wonderfully sweet," responded **Anansi**. And he immediately began to think of how he could get some of that **soup** for his own **lunch**.

Anansi was still thinking, when **Tiger** said to him, "Hand me that **coconut** over there, **Anansi**. I'm going to add it to my **soup**."

And so, **Anansi** handed **Tiger** the **coconut**. This is the sign for **coconut,** and this is the sign for **banana**. Can you do these signs with me? Great!

Tiger added the **coconut** to his **soup** and then turned to **Anansi,** "Anansi, while you are just standing there, pass me that bunch of **bananas**. Bananas will taste great in my **soup**."

After some time had passed **Anansi** said, "Friend **Tiger,** it's really a hot day. Would you like to go **swimming** with me? We could take a nice dip in the river while our **soup** cools."

"*Our* soup?! This is *my* soup!" shouted Tiger. "And you know I don't ever go swimming. No, thank you, **Anansi.** I will stay here with *my* **soup."**

"Excuse me, **Tiger.** Of course it's your **soup,**" replied **Anansi** in a kindly tone. "And I will teach you how to swim. It's easy. Come on, let's go."

Tiger thought a minute and then said, "Well, my **soup** is rather hot. I guess it wouldn't hurt to walk down to the river with you while it cools."

And so off they went. When they arrived at the river, **Anansi** said, "Now **Tiger,** all you have to do is close your eyes and jump in. Swimming is easy because all you do is let the water hold you up. I'll count to five for you and on five, you close your eyes and jump in."

"Oh, no **Anansi,**" answered **Tiger** "That's one of your tricks. We'll jump in at the same time. I will count to five and you jump in with me."

Then **Tiger** closed his eyes and began counting. As soon as Tiger's eyes were closed, **Anansi** bent down and picked up the biggest rock he could see. When **Tiger** got to "five" he jumped in. At the same moment, **Anansi** threw the rock in the river as hard as he could and then he ran back to **Tiger's soup.** He gobbled it all up as fast as he could.

Tiger floated around for awhile and then called to **Anansi,** "Anansi, where are you? This water is nice. I like it. From now on I will always go swimming while my soup cools. **Anansi,** where are you? **Anansi**?"

But **Anansi** had scurried off through the woods to find a hiding place. He knew that **Tiger** would come looking for him. Along the way, he saw some **monkeys** playing a singing game on the ground, and that gave **Anansi** an idea.

"Would you like to learn a new song?" he asked the **monkeys.**

"Yes! Yes!" they all cried.

Here are the signs for **monkey, lunch, afternoon** and **song.** Let's do these signs together.

"Here is how the new **song** goes," explained **Anansi.** "And here is the dance that goes with it. Sing and dance it with me as soon as you know my new **song.**" *(to the tune of "Farmer in the Dell")*

> *This **afternoon** for lunch,*
> *We ate the Tiger's soup.*
> *Hi, ho this **afternoon**,*
> *We ate the Tiger's soup.*

The **monkeys** sang this **song** over and over again. Then **Anansi** said, "Here is the second verse. Sing it with me as soon as you know it."

> *Coconuts in the soup.*
> *We ate the Tiger's lunch.*
> *Hi, ho banana soup,*
> *We ate the Tiger's lunch.*

The **monkeys** were having such a good time singing and dancing their new **song** that they didn't notice that **Anansi** had slipped away into the forest.

Meanwhile, **Tiger** had finished swimming and had gone back to eat his fine **soup** for **lunch.** When he saw the empty pot, he was furiously angry. He thought that **Anansi** had tricked him once again and had set out to find him when he heard singing. **Tiger** stopped and listened. He heard a **song,** and it was a song about his missing **lunch!**

> *This **afternoon** for lunch,*
> *We ate the Tiger's soup.*
> *Hi, ho this **afternoon**,*
> *We ate the Tiger's soup."*

> *Coconuts in the soup.*
> *We ate the Tiger's lunch.*
> *Hi, ho banana soup,*
> *We ate the Tiger's lunch.*

"**Monkeys,** just listen to my **song,**" Tiger roared.

> *This **afternoon** for lunch.*
> *I'll eat the Monkeys up.*
> *Hi, ho, this **afternoon***
> *I'll eat the Monkeys up.*

Quickly the **monkeys** climbed up in the tree tops where **Tiger** couldn't catch them. There the **monkeys** were safe. **Tiger** never did find out that it was **Anansi** who had eaten his **soup.**

And ever since that time, **monkeys** have always lived in tree tops and **tigers** have always loved swimming in rivers and trying to catch **monkeys** for their lunch.

Anansi Drinks Boiling Water

1 Anansi the Spider did not like work. He was always trying to figure out ways to get food for himself and his family without doing any more work than he needed to, and this story is about one of the ways he came up with.

One day, the king ordered all the animals in his kingdom to report the next morning to his fields to dig up all the yams and carry them to his storehouse.

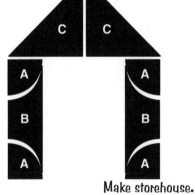

Make storehouse.

2 Now, Anansi saw this as an opportunity to get yams for himself. So that night he dug a big hole at the side of the field and covered it up with sticks and grass.

Make hole.

All that next day, the animals worked digging up yams and carrying them to the king's storehouse. The animals were very surprised to see Anansi there working

along with them in the fields. But, of course, Anansi was really working for himself. For each yam Anansi carried to the king's storehouse, he quietly and secretly dropped one into his special hole.

3 Late that night, after all the animals had gone home, Anansi came back to the field and carried the king's stolen yams one by one to his own home. Then he went back and filled in the hole.

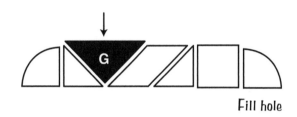

Fill hole

4 Morning came and word began to spread that Anansi had a house full of yams. Of course, everyone knew Anansi had stolen the yams, but no one could prove it.

Finally even the king heard about Anansi's houseful of yams, and he called Anansi to his palace. The king said, "Anansi, you have a houseful of yams and everyone thinks you stole those yams from my fields."

Make king.

"No, no," Anansi protested. "You all saw me working as hard as everyone else yesterday. Everyone saw me in your fields carrying yams to your storehouse."

"Anansi, you are known to be a trickster, and a very good one at that," the king answered. "You have tricked everyone here at one time or another. And now, your house is full of yams, when only yesterday you had nothing at all to eat. I cannot prove that you are guilty of stealing my yams, but I have decided that you must prove to me that you are innocent."

"Fine, fine. I am innocent. How can I prove it to you king?" said Anansi.

The king declared, "You must drink boiling water. If you are innocent, then the water will not hurt you. But if you are guilty of stealing my yams, the boiling water will scald your mouth. And everyone will watch the test to make sure you do not try another trick." Then the king called everyone to gather around the cookstove.

Anansi thought for a minute and then said, "Very well, then. Pour some boiling water for me to drink and I will prove that I am innocent."

5

The king's servant poured the boiling water into a cup.

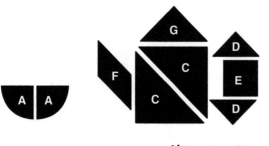

Make pot and cup.

Anansi pretended to taste the water and right away he said, "This water is not hot enough. Let's put it in the hot sun so that the sun will make it hotter."

Anansi knew that if he put the water in the sunlight, it would stop boiling and begin to cool down.

All the animals agreed to the plan, and Anansi carried the water out into the sunlight. Every few minutes, he would go out to check on it, always coming back into the shade where the other animals waited saying, "Not hot enough yet. I must drink really hot water so I can prove to you that I did not steal the yams."

All the animals agreed. Finally, Anansi came back into the shade carrying the hot water. He announced, "Now I am ready to drink this boiling hot water to prove my innocence. But first, I want to pass the cup around so that everyone may look and see that the water is the very same water that the king's servant poured."

Anansi knew that by passing the cup around, the water would cool down even more. All the animals passed the cup of hot water around. When the cup finally got back to Anansi, he took a deep breath and drank it all in one gulp. And he shouted, "See, I am innocent!"

6

Then Anansi went home to his house full of the king's yams!

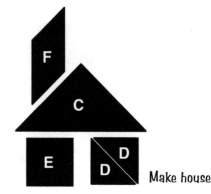

Make house

10

Anansi Goes Bald

Anansi is a spider who is known as a trickster. He is usually trying to trick one of his fellow earth creatures into giving him something for free. Anansi is rather lazy and spends lots of time trying to get out of work that he should be doing.

But Anansi isn't all bad. Often he tries to be good and to help others. Sometimes, though, even when his intentions are the best, he gets sidetracked. In this story, Anansi's stomach gets in the way of his good intentions.

One morning Anansi woke up and decided that he would help someone. He said, "Now, who shall I help? I want to be good and help someone today. Ah, I know, I will help Granny. She needs to plant her garden, but it is hard for her because she is so old. I will offer to plant her garden for her."

So Anansi walked to Granny's house and he called, "Granny, oh Granny, are you home? I've come to plant your garden today."

Granny came out when she heard Anansi. "Why Anansi, that's wonderful," she said. "You must be having one of your good days. I would love for you to plant my garden. Right now, I'm making Hot Beans for lunch. When you are finished hoeing the garden, you may knock on my door, and I will serve you a bowl. Would you like that?"

"Yeah!! Yeah!!," exclaimed Anansi. "Hot Beans are my favorite food. I will start hoeing your garden right away."

So Anansi put his hat over his beautiful head of hair and walked out to the garden. He hoed very hard in nice straight rows—for a while! **(Cut 1 to 2.)** That is, until he began to catch the delicious smell of Granny's Hot Beans coming from her kitchen. His hoeing

slowed and the row became crooked. **(Cut 2 to 3, leg.)** Finally, Anansi stopped working—so that he could smell better, you understand. He leaned on his hoe and just sniffed and sniffed the wonderful aroma coming from the kitchen. Can you sniff with your nose like Anansi did?

Then Anansi remembered that he was supposed to be hoeing and he started working again. He hoed very hard in nice straight rows —for a while. That is, until he thought about the delicious taste of Granny's Hot Beans. His hoeing slowed and the row became crooked again. **(Cut 3 to 4, leg.)** Finally, Anansi stopped working—so that he could taste better, you understand. He leaned on his hoe and just smacked his lips and smacked his lips. Can you smack your lips like Anansi did?

Then Anansi remembered that he was supposed to be hoeing and he started working again. He hoed very hard in nice straight rows —for a while. That is, until he thought about the wonderful sound of Granny's Hot Beans cooking. His hoeing slowed and the row became crooked again. **(Cut 4 to 5, leg.)** Finally, Anansi stopped working—so that he could hear better, you understand. He leaned on his hoe and cupped his ears with both his hands. Can you cup your ears like Anansi did?

Then Anansi remembered that he was supposed to be hoeing and he started working again. He hoed very hard in nice straight rows —for a while. That is, until he thought about the glorious sight of Granny's Hot Beans. His hoeing slowed, and the row became crooked again. **(Cut from 5 to 6.)** Finally, Anansi stopped working—so that he could see better, you understand. He leaned on his hoe, shaded his eyes with both hands and squinted to see Granny's Hot Beans. Can you shade your eyes and lean forward to see the bubbling beans like Anansi did?

Now—all this time that Anansi had been hoeing and smelling; all this time that Anansi had been hoeing and smacking; all this time that Anansi had been hoeing and listening; all this time that Anansi had been hoeing and seeing Granny's Hot Beans—you know—Anansi had been creeping closer and closer to Granny's house. *(Encourage children to act all these motions out again with you.)*

By the time Anansi thought that he could see Granny's Hot Beans, he was practically right up to her kitchen window. So Anansi quickly finished the hoeing with a little chop-chop here and a little chop-chop there. **(Cut 7, mouth.)** He didn't really do a very good job and the ground was all jagged and bumpy like this. **(Cut 6 to 8, hair.)**

And here is Anansi, **(Unfold cut-out and show spider.)** and this is Anansi's hair. Yes, you can imagine how proud Anansi was of his beautiful thick hair. Every so often, he'd pull out his comb, take off his hat and just comb his beautiful thick hair. He liked it to stick straight up so that everyone would notice it. **(Stroke Anansi's hair.)** Anyway, Anansi found himself standing at Granny's door. He pulled out his comb and took off his hat. He fixed up his hair and put his hat back on. Then he knocked softly on Granny's door. *(Invite the children to knock softly with you.)* He called out quietly in his sweetest voice, "Please, Granny, it's me, Anansi. Please, I'm all done with the hoeing. Please can I have some of your wonderful Hot Beans now? Please?"

Anansi thought that if he asked really nicely and said please several times that maybe Granny would give him an extra big helping. There was no answer. So Anansi tried again. *(Invite the children to knock louder with you and ask this a little louder.)* He knocked at Granny's door a little louder and called out a little louder in his sweetest voice, "Please, Granny, it's me, Anansi. Please, I'm all done with the hoeing. Please can I have some of your wonderful Hot Beans now? Please?"

Still there was no answer. Then Anansi remembered that Granny appeared to be quite deaf at times. So he tried one more time in his loudest but sweetest voice. *(Can you knock loudly and say this with me in a very loud voice?)* "Please, Granny, it's me, Anansi. Please, I'm all done with the hoeing. Please have can I have some of your wonderful Hot Beans now? *Please?*"

Still there was no answer. Granny was obviously not at home. So what do you think Anansi did next? *(Ask for children's ideas.)* That's right. Anansi decided to go into Granny's house and get some of those good Hot Beans for himself. He looked all around him to see if anyone was watching. *(Look around you.)*

Then he quickly opened Granny's door and went in. He walked over to the stove.

Yup! There were those Hot Beans, bubbling in a big pot. They looked and smelled and sounded just as delicious as Anansi thought they would. He just *had* to taste some. Besides, he deserved it. After all, he did hoe Granny's garden… well, some of the garden at least. Okay…. so he had hoed only a little. He had spent most of his time leaning on his hoe. But Granny wouldn't mind if he had some Hot Beans… or would she?

Anansi tasted a little spoonful. Yum! They were so delicious. He tasted another spoonful… and then another. Then he started to worry. What if Granny came back and found him standing at her stove and eating her Hot Beans straight out of her pot!?

Anansi Goes Bald

Anansi knew how mad Granny could get, so he decided to just take some of her Hot Beans and leave as quickly as he could. But what could he put the Hot Beans in? If he used one of her bowls, she would know for sure. What should he use? *(Ask for ideas from the children.)*

Yes, Anansi decided to put the Hot Beans in his hat. That way Granny would never know he had taken them. So Anansi dipped Hot Beans into his hat as fast as he could. Then he started walking toward the door. But who do you think walked in right at that minute? Yes, it was Granny. Anansi quickly put his hat behind his back.

Anansi said in his sweetest voice, "Why hello, Granny. I was just going to…. ahh, going to… ahh, I was just going to get myself a nice tall glass of cool water. I've been hard at work all morning. You know that sun is awfully hot when you hoe as hard as I do. I didn't think you'd mind me helping myself to some of your cool water. By the way, your Hot Beans smell delicious. If you don't mind, I'll come back after I'm all done working in your garden, and then perhaps you could give me a bowlful like you promised. I'd be happy with even a small bowlful of your delicious Hot Beans."

All the time that Anansi was talking, he was walking backwards towards the door just as fast as he could. Granny smiled sweetly at Anansi and said, "Why certainly, Anansi. I'd be happy to share my Hot Beans with you. You are really a dear to hoe my garden for me."

Oh, Anansi was so relieved to hear Granny say that. Anansi thought she hadn't noticed that he has hiding his hat behind his back and he was just about to the door.

Then Granny called out sweetly, "Anansi, dear, put your hat on before you go out in the sun. It doesn't do you much good behind your back like that. You know, that sun can be awfully hot when you hoe as hard as you do."

What could Anansi do but put on his hat? No one ever disobeyed Granny.

As soon as Anansi put his hat on, Hot Beans started to run down his head. Anansi didn't know how hot those Hot Beans were. They were hot, hot, hot! They burned his head so badly that smoke started coming out of his ears. He started shaking and dancing all around Granny's kitchen.

"What are you doing there, dearie?" Granny asked Anansi.

"I'm doing the Hat-Shakin' Dance. It will help me hoe your garden better," he answered as he dashed out of the house just as fast as he could.

As soon as he was out of sight of the house, Anansi jerked off his hat and rubbed all the Hot Beans off his head. But Anansi's beautiful thick hair came off too. Those Hot Beans had burned every hair off of Anansi's head! **(#9, cut hair off.)** His head was shiny!

And that's why spiders are bald and shiny today!

13

ANANSI GOES BALD

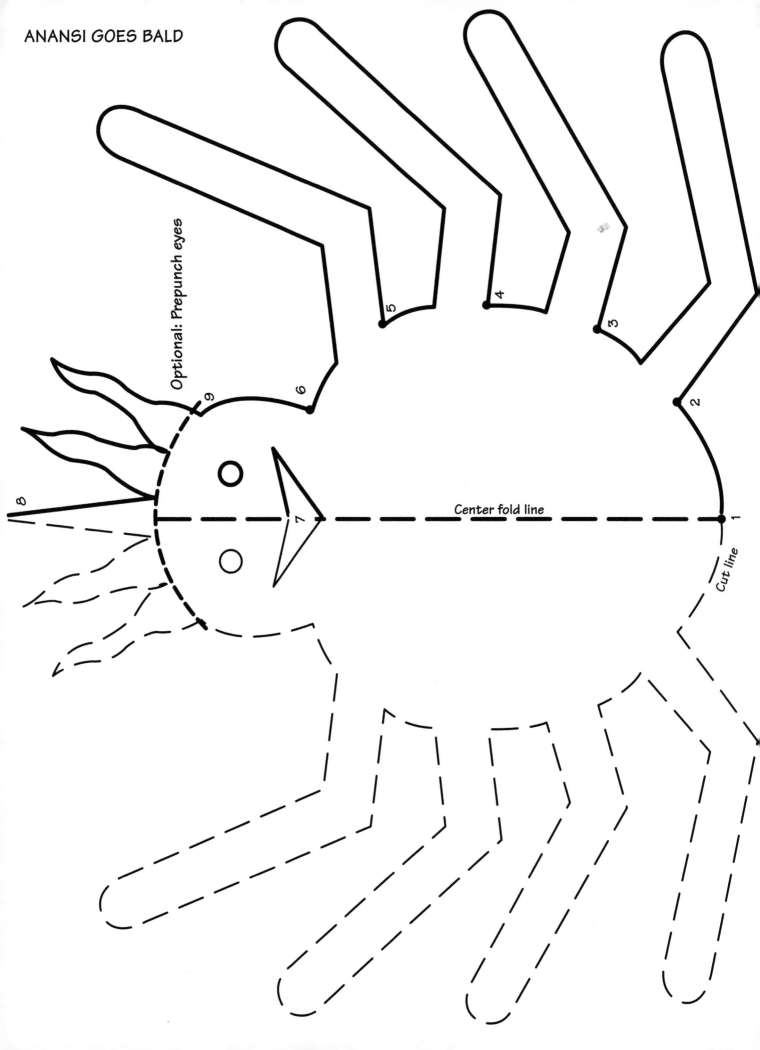

Optional: Prepunch eyes

Center fold line

Cut line

Anansi's Last Trick

Anansi is a trickster who is always out looking for an easy way to get his next lunch. In this story, Anansi ends up tricking himself.

Far ago Anansi was traveling through a country that was ruled by a mean queen. Most of the time the inhabitants of this country called her Queen. But some of the time they called her Five, that is when they wanted to make her angry. Five was the queen's real name, and she absolutely hated it. And everyone knew it. But what they didn't know was that their queen was a witch who could make very strong magic spells.

Because she hated her name so much, Queen Five decided to put an evil curse on the word "Five." Anyone who said the word, would immediately fall down dead.

Anansi found out about this curse. How did he find out?

Anansi, being the nosy sort of fellow that he was, just happened to be standing outside Queen Five's back fence as she was cooking her magic brew. She chanted magic words to turn the word "five" into a "say-it-and-fall-down-dead" word.

Anansi scurried away, thinking to himself, "I'm the only one besides the Queen who knows this secret about the word fi.... oh I can't say the word or I'll be dead. How can I turn this secret into lunch?" Anansi was always thinking about his next lunch.

Anansi got an idea. He carried all of his yams (sweet potatoes) down to the river where all the animals had to come to get a drink. He put them in five small piles. **(#1 Write numerals 1 to 5 across bottom of paper.)** Then Anansi sat down next to his yam piles and waited.

Pretty soon a rabbit came hopping along. Anansi called out, "Hello there, Rabbit. Fine day for a drink of water, isn't it?"

Rabbit thought this was a very strange question but she answered politely. "Why yes, it is. But then every day is a good day for a drink of water."

"Say, Rabbit," continued Anansi, "I was wondering if you could help me out a little. I've got these piles of yams here and I just can't seem to get them counted correctly. Could you please tell me how many yam piles I have?" **(#2 Draw Rabbit.)**

Rabbit answered, "Why certainly Anansi. That's easy." Rabbit started to count. "One, two, three, four, five." *(Point to each numeral as you say it. Children may help count.)*

As soon as Rabbit said "five" she fell down dead.

Anansi ran over and gobbled her up. He said, "Boy, that was a great lunch!" *(Fold Rabbit down on herself.)*

Pretty soon a duck came waddling along. Anansi called out, "Hello there, Duck. Fine day for a drink of water, isn't it?"

Duck thought this was a very strange question but he answered politely. "Why yes, it is. But then every day is a good day for a drink of water."

"Say, Duck," continued Anansi, "I was wondering if you could help me out a little. I've got these piles of yams here and I just can't seem to get them counted correctly. Could you please tell me how many yam piles I have?" **(#3 Draw Duck.)**

Duck answered, "Why certainly Anansi. That's easy." Duck started to count. "One, two, three, four, five." *(Point to each numeral as you say it. Children may help count.)*

As soon as Duck said "five" he fell down dead. *(Fold Duck over on itself.)*

Anansi ran over and gobbled him up. He said, "Boy, that was a great lunch!"

Pretty soon another animal came walking along. What animal do you think came along next? *(You can use the pig or let listeners choose their own animal.)* **(#4 Draw Pig.)** Here is our *Pig*.

Anansi called out, "Hello there *Pig*. Fine day for a drink of water, isn't it?"

Pig thought this was a very strange question but he answered politely. "Why yes, it is. But then every day is a good day for a drink of water."

"Say, *Pig*," Anansi continued, "I was wondering if you could help me out a little. I've got these piles of yams here and I just can't seem to get them counted correctly. Could you please tell me how many yam piles I have?"

Pig answered, "Why certainly, Anansi. That's easy." *Pig* started to count, "One, two, three, four, and the one I'm sitting on."

"No, no," protested Anansi. "That's not the way you count it. Try it again."

So *Pig* counted again the exact same way. "One, two, three, four, and the one I'm sitting on."

And again Anansi said, "No, no. That's not the way you count it. Try it again."

So *Pig* counted again the exact same way. "One, two, three, four, and the one I'm sitting on."

Finally, Anansi got so angry that he said to *Pig*, "You are not doing it right. Let me show you how to count these piles of yams. Now watch this." **(#5 Draw spider.)**

Anansi began to count. He yelled, "One, two, three, four, five!" And course, as soon as Anansi yelled "five," he fell down dead. And that was the end of Anansi… and that is the end of this story.

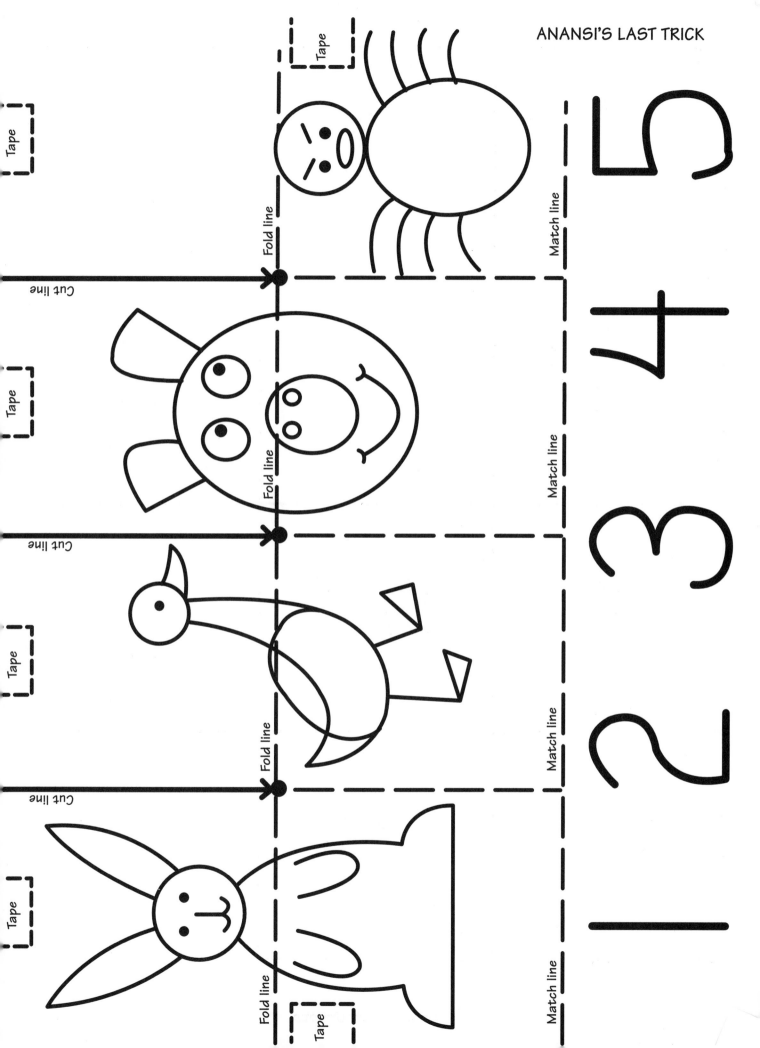

ANANSI'S LAST TRICK

Coyote	**Turkey**	**Tree**
Place RH tips around nose, then draw away into flat "O."	Place back of RH "Q" against nose, then shake down.	RH "5"-shaped, palm left. Put RH elbow on back of LH, then shake RH.
Chop (tree)	**Wood**	**Fire**
LH "5"-shaped. Chop LH wrist with little-finger side of RH.	Slide little-finger side of RH "W"-shaped back and forth on left wrist as if sawing wood.	"Five"-shape both hands, palms in. Move upward.
Cook	**Eat**	**Sit**
Open "B"-shape both hands. Place RH palm down on LH, palm up. Flip RH over as if flipping pancakes.	Circle RH "A" to mouth, as if eating.	"H"-shape both hands. Lower RH onto LH.
There	**Wait**	
Point RH index finger out.	Hold out open hands, palms up. LH a little ahead of RH, wiggle fingers slightly.	

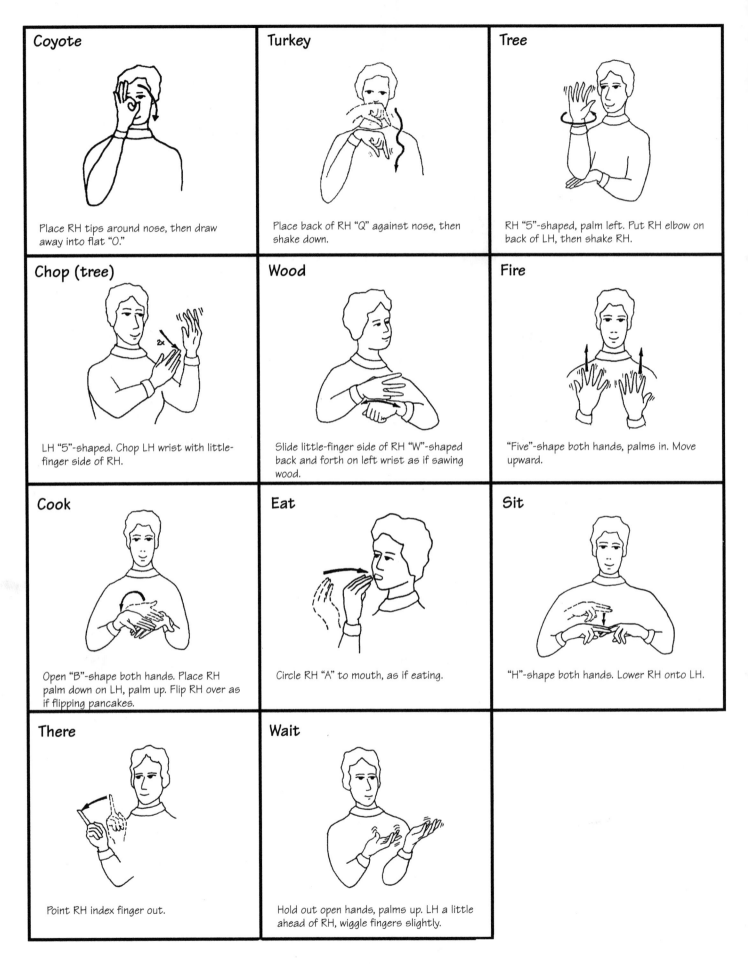

Turkey Tricks Coyote

Turkey Tricks Coyote

Coyote is a famous trickster from the American West. He is everybody's favorite loser. He thinks of ways to fool his friends, and is always trying to cheat them out of their lunch.

But many of Coyote's schemes backfire and he himself gets tricked. In this story, Coyote is outsmarted by another animal, Turkey.

Far ago, Coyote caught Turkey. He was so hungry, he opened his mouth to take a big juicy bite out of Turkey.

But Turkey said, "Wait a minute there, Mr. Coyote. Do you really mean to eat me cold? I would taste much better if you roasted me over a nice roaring fire, now wouldn't I?"

Coyote, who was not real bright, replied, "You are right. But how would I get the firewood?"

Turkey pointed to the nearest tree and answered, "What about this tree? Just use it for firewood. Doesn't a nice hot turkey sandwich sound great?"

Coyote said, "How can I use this tree for firewood? It's growing in the ground."

Turkey answered, "Coyote, I can't believe you asked that. All you have to do is chop the tree down."

Coyote answered, "Chop the tree down. Good idea. But how do I do that? I am holding onto you. If I put you down so I can chop the tree, you will get away."

Turkey answered, "Coyote, you can trust me. I won't fly away. You know I can't even fly very well. I'll just sit in the tree while you are chopping it down. That way you'll know just where I am."

Coyote answered, "Good idea. Now, promise me you'll stay up in the tree while I'm chopping it."

Turkey said, "I promise."

So Coyote let Turkey go and Turkey flew up into the tree.

Coyote started chopping with his ax.

But in about two minutes, Coyote started to get tired. He said, "Turkey, you come down out of that tree. Chopping this tree down is too much work. I'll just eat you cold."

Turkey said, "No, no. I'll taste so much better hot. Just keep chopping. I'll sing a little song about you. That will make your chopping so much easier."

Coyote said, "A song about me?! No one has ever sung a song about me before!"

Turkey sang to Coyote as he chopped. *(Sung to the tune of "Turkey in the Straw." Add signs for bolded terms to introduce the actions to children.)*

> ***Coyote, chop*** *this* ***tree.***
> ***Coyote, chop*** *this* ***tree.***
> *Use this* ***wood*** *to light your* ***fire.***
> *Then you* ***cook me*** *and* ***eat*** *me up.*

We can all sing this song with Turkey. Let's learn the signs. Here are the signs for **Coyote, chop, tree.** Try these signs with me. Here are the signs for **wood** and **fire.** Let's try these signs. Here are the signs for **cook, me,** and **eat.** Let's do these. Great! Now we can sing the entire song.

Turkey sat in the tree and sang while Coyote chopped Turkey's tree. Let's sing Turkey's song.

> ***Coyote, chop*** *this* ***tree.***
> ***Coyote, chop*** *this* ***tree.***
> *Use this* ***wood*** *to light your* ***fire.***
> *Then you* ***cook me*** *and* ***eat*** *me up.*

Turkey sang and sang to Coyote. He sang as if this was the most important song in the world. But after all, Turkey never did anything all day anyway, so sitting in a tree and singing a silly song over and over was just fine with him. After a while Coyote said, "Turkey, that is a mighty fine song you are singing, and it does help me chop faster. But you know I also am a good singer. Listen to my song. I just made it up."

Coyote sang his song. *(Sung to the tune of "Turkey in the Straw." Add signs.)* It went like this.

> *Turkey in the tree.*
> *Turkey in the tree.*
> *Sit right there and wait for me,*
> *Sit right there while I chop this tree.*

We can sing Coyote's song with him. Here are the signs for **Turkey, sit, there,** and **wait.** You already know the signs for **tree, me,** and **chop.** Let's sing Coyote's song together.

> *Turkey in the tree.*
> *Turkey in the tree.*
> *Sit right there and wait for me,*
> *Sit right there while I chop this tree.*

Turkey said, "Coyote, that is a really nice song. I love it. But I think my song is better. Listen to it again." Turkey sang his song again.

> *Coyote, chop this tree.*
> *Coyote, chop this tree.*
> *Use this wood to light your fire.*
> *Then you cook me and eat me up.*

Coyote said, "Turkey, that is a really nice song. But mine is better. Listen to it again." Coyote sang his song again.

> *Turkey in the tree.*
> *Turkey in the tree.*
> *Sit right there and wait for me,*
> *Sit right there while I chop this tree.*

Turkey and Coyote argued and sang, sang and argued about whose song was better. And each time they sang their song, they sang faster and louder and louder and faster. *(Depending on your listeners, you could encourage them to sing and sign both songs louder and faster. Or you could divide the listeners into two groups. One group could sing Turkey's song and one group could sing Coyote's song.)*

Now in between all this singing, Coyote was still chopping down the tree that Turkey was sitting in. Just as the tree was about to fall, Turkey flew to another tree. Turkey started singing his song again. *(Repeat refrain.)*

Coyote knew just what to do. He got busy chopping on the new tree. Coyote sang his song to Turkey. Turkey sang his song to Coyote. They sang louder and faster. They sang faster and louder. Coyote chopped and chopped. Just as the tree was about to fall, Turkey flew to another tree.

Coyote knew just what to do. He got busy chopping on the new tree. Coyote sang his song to Turkey. Turkey sang his song to Coyote. They sang louder and faster. They sang faster and louder. Coyote chopped and chopped. Just as the tree was about to fall, Turkey flew to another tree. *(Repeat this sequence as many times as desired.)*

By the end of the day, Coyote was dog-tired, Coyote was exhausted, Coyote was pooped, Coyote was weary. Coyote could not chop any more trees. He could not sing his song anymore. Coyote was laying on the ground half-dead.

And Turkey flew away home.

Coyote's Flying Lesson

Coyote is a famous trickster in the American Southwest. He is known as a very cunning and conniving thief who can be quite a nuisance to his fellow creatures. Nevertheless, they admire him because of the clever ways that he survives the trouble he is always getting himself into.

Far ago, Coyote was going along looking for some new trouble. (**#1 Draw coyote outline.**) And he found it! He found trouble with the black crows. (**#2 and #3 Draw ears.**) Here's what happened:

Coyote saw all the black crows gathered in one place. (**#4 Draw jaw.**) They were singing loudly and dancing wildly. Coyote thought it looked like fun. (**#5 Draw teeth.**)

At the end of their dance, the crows took off into the sky. They flew around in large circles. (**#6 Draw hind leg.**)

They flew around in small circles. (**#7 Draw eyes.**) They flew straight up. (**#8 Draw front leg.**) They flew straight down. (**#9 Draw stomach.**)

It looked like so much fun that Coyote wanted to fly too.

He called to the crows, "Hey crows, old buddies, old pals, friends of mine, teach me to fly. Will you? If I know how to fly, then I will be the greatest coyote in all the world."

The crows cawed to each other. "Listen to Coyote. Now he says he is our friend. Now he wants us to teach him to fly. What do you say, shall we teach him to fly?"

The crows remembered that Coyote had pulled some pretty nasty tricks on them not too long ago, and they were still very angry with him, but now they agreed to teach him to fly. Do you think the crows might be planning to pull a trick of their own on Coyote?

The crows flew down to Coyote and circled around him.

"Fly? You want to fly?" they called. "How much do you want to fly, Coyote, old buddy, old pal? Would you like some of our feathers?"

"Yeah, yeah, yeah!!" Coyote said, "I really want to fly! I want to be the greatest coyote in all the world. Teach me to fly. Please? Pretty please?"

And then one of the crows pulled a feather from his wing. He stuck it into Coyote's back as hard as he could. (**#10 Draw feather on Coyote's back.**)

"Ouch!" yelped Coyote, "Oh, I mean, I'm learning to fly."

Another one of the crows pulled a feather from his wing. He stuck it into Coyote's back as hard as he could. (**#11 Draw feather.**)

"Ouch!" yelped Coyote, "Oh, I mean, I'm learning to fly."

Then another one of the crows pulled a feather from his wing. He stuck it into Coyote's back as hard as he could. (**#12 Draw feather.**)

"Ouch!" yelped Coyote, "Oh, I mean, I'm learning to fly."

A fourth crow pulled a feather from his wing. He stuck it into Coyote's back as hard as he could. (**#13 Draw feather.**)

"Ouch!" yelped Coyote, "Oh, I mean, I'm learning to fly." (*Continue this with as many feathers as desired.*)

Finally Coyote was completely covered with feathers. The crows said, "Coyote, you are ready to sing and dance with us."

"No, I want to fly! Fly, I say!" cried Coyote.

And together the crows answered, "No, first you sing and then you dance. Then you fly."

So Coyote sang as loudly as he could. He danced as wildly as he could. He thought that if he was very loud and very obnoxious, the crows would get tired of it and teach him to fly sooner. He was right.

The crows crowded in around Coyote and lifted him onto their wings. All at once the entire group took off into the air.

There was Coyote, right in the middle of the crows. They held onto him and flew him around in large circles. (**#14 Draw large circle.**) They held onto him and flew him around in small circles. (**#15 Draw small circle.**) They held onto him and flew him straight up. (**#16 Draw leg line up.**) They held onto him and flew him straight down. (**#17 Draw leg line down.**)

Coyote said, "Move away I say, you old crows. I have feathers. Let me fly on my own."

So the crows flew away from Coyote. Coyote flapped his legs up and down, even though the feathers were on his back. He shouted, "Look at me. I am the greatest Coyote in the world. I am flying!"

And though he flapped his legs as hard as he could, Coyote began to fall very slowly to the ground.

"Hey crows! Help me! I can't fly anymore. Help!" he called.

The crows flew over to him.

"Well, it's about time." Coyote complained. "You all said you would teach me to fly, so teach me—before I hit the ground!"

The crows answered, "We never said we would teach you to fly. We just gave you feathers. And now we want our feathers back."

One crow flew over Coyote and plucked out a feather. (**Cut off feather #13.**)

A second crow flew over Coyote and plucked out a feather. (**Cut off feather #12.**)

A third crow flew over Coyote and plucked out a feather. (**Cut off feather #11.**)

The fourth crow flew over Coyote and plucked out a feather. (**Cut off feather #10.**)

Coyote fell to the ground. *Splat!* He landed in a mud puddle. Coyote struggled to his feet, lifted his head and began to yell at the crows who were cawing at him from high up in the sky.

From that day on, Coyote has called into the night sky, howling for the crows to come back and teach him to fly.

Today, Coyote is still the color of mud and he still can't fly. But that old Coyote, he is still out there looking for trouble.

COYOTE'S FLYING LESSON

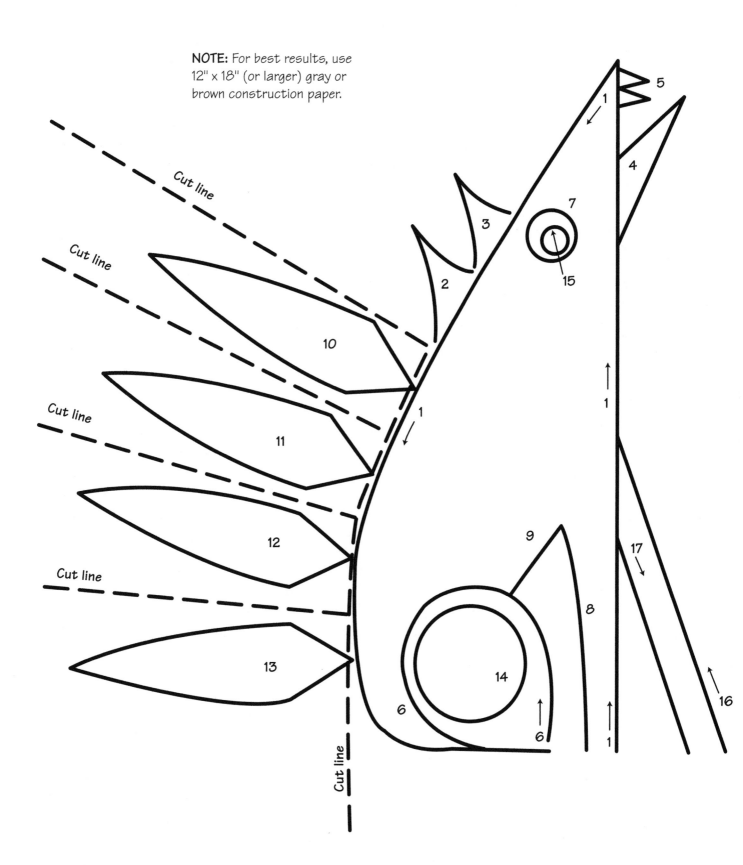

NOTE: For best results, use 12" x 18" (or larger) gray or brown construction paper.

Coyote Tricks Rabbit–
Or Does He?

Coyote and Rabbit are both tricksters in many stories. In this story, they are both the tricksters and the victims.

Far ago, Coyote was eating his lunch. But you know Coyote, and you know that it was not really *his* lunch that he was eating. No, Coyote was stealing his lunch out of a farmer's garden.

Coyote has never been very smart. You can figure out that Coyote should have been keeping an eye out for the farmer while he was stealing the farmer's vegetables. But he wasn't. The farmer quietly snuck up on Coyote and grabbed him.

"What are you doing? Why did you grab me? I was in your garden because I was just going to pick your delicious green beans for you, Mr. Farmer, sir," Coyote said with his mouth full of beans. **(#1 Draw two beans.)**

The farmer said, "Oh, no, Coyote. I know you better than that. You were stealing my food. You've done it before, haven't you? But this time I've caught you, and I'm not letting you get away from me. I'm going to have you for my lunch!"

And with that, the farmer stuffed Coyote in a sack and hung him up on his fence. Then he built a big fire. He said, "Coyote, I am going to make you into Coyote soup! Look at this big pot! Think you will fit into that?! Ha, ha!" **(#2 Draw pot.)**

Coyote replied, "I know Mr. Farmer sir, that you are a very good cook. But I am rather old and stringy. Even with all your cooking skills, I am afraid that I will not taste very good. You would enjoy me so much more if you added some salt, pepper and spices to your Coyote soup."

The farmer said, "You are right Coyote. I will go get some salt and pepper. Why don't you just 'hang around' until I get back? Get it? Hang around! Ha, ha."

The farmer went off and Coyote started to think fast. But Rabbit came hopping along before Coyote had even thought of his next trick!

Coyote called out to Rabbit, "Rabbit, how are you this cold and frosty day. Unusually cold out today, don't you think?"

Rabbit said, "Coyote, come to think of it, I am rather cold. But just what are you doing hanging in the farmer's bag on the fence?"

"Hanging in the bag?" responded Coyote. "Why, ah, I am keeping warm in here. This is a nice warm bag, and the farmer is letting me borrow it. You look so cold Rabbit."

"Yes, I am cold. But Coyote, why are you hanging on the fence?" asked Rabbit.

Coyote answered, "Hanging on the fence? Why, ah, the farmer, he built me a fire to keep me warm. I asked him to let me hang up here in the fire's warmth. Hot air rises you know, and it is much warmer up here than standing on the cold, cold ground. Your feet do look cold, Rabbit."

Rabbit answered, "Come to think of it, my feet are rather cold. But, Coyote, why is the pot on the fire? It is full of boiling water."

Coyote answered, "The pot? Why, ah, the farmer, he put a pot of water on to boil so that we could have some nice hot tea. By the way, Rabbit, you look like you could use a nice hot cup of tea." **(#3 Draw handle on mug.)**

Rabbit answered, "Yes, I am cold enough for a cup of hot tea. I wish I was warm like you."

Coyote answered, "Warm like me? Rabbit, since we are such good friends and have known each other for such a long time, I will let you trade places with me. It is just for this once, and I don't think that the farmer will mind."

Rabbit said, "Oh, would you trade places with me?! Here, let me lift the bag down so that you can get out, Coyote. Then I can climb in your nice warm bag."

Rabbit lifted the bag down and Coyote was out in a flash. Rabbit climbed in the bag. He lifted Rabbit up on the fence and ran away, yelling, "Enjoy the farmer's hot water for me, will you Rabbit?"

When the farmer came back and saw that Coyote had tricked Rabbit into the bag, he decided to cook Rabbit instead. But Rabbit was so angry at Coyote for tricking him that his anger gave him extra strength and energy to squirm furiously away from the farmer and run after Coyote.

Rabbit found Coyote asleep near a tree. While Coyote slept, Rabbit found a big bee hive and very, very carefully set it down next to Coyote. He waited for Coyote to wake up. Soon Coyote did wake up. He saw the bee hive and he saw Rabbit. He asked, "What's this, Rabbit?"

Rabbit answered, "Why Coyote, that is a little school. Everyday I take care of the tiny children and teach them, but just now I have to go. Could you be the teacher for me? You would be good at it."

Coyote said, "I don't know anything about teaching. What do I have to do?"

Rabbit answered, "All you have to do is make sure that all the tiny children stay in their school. It is their rest time, you see. If one of them tries to come out, just give the school a little tap with this stick. That will teach the others to stay inside."

Coyote said, "Well, that sounds easy enough. But hurry back, Rabbit."

Rabbit hopped away as fast as he could. Coyote sat there with his stick ready. Soon one tiny child flew out of the little school. (**#4 Draw small oval above mug.**) Coyote loved hitting things with a stick, so he whacked the little school as hard as he could.

Then another tiny child came out. (**#5 Draw another circle above mug.**) Again Coyote whacked the school as hard as he could. (What was the child? Yes, it was a bumblebee. What was the little school? Yes, it was the bee hive.) After the second whack, all the tiny children flew out of their hive. They were mad, very mad. They all flew at Coyote and what do you think they did to him? Yes, they stung him many, many times. (**#6 Draw more bees coming out.**) Rabbit really tricked Coyote back, didn't he?

It took Coyote a few days to recover from all those bee stings, and during that time he had lots of time to think of another trick to pull on Rabbit. (**Fold paper at line A so that only handle shows.**)

Coyote knew of a place on the mountain where the rock formed an arch. He waited there for Rabbit.

As soon as he heard Rabbit hopping along, he quickly positioned himself under the rock. He looked like this. (**#7 Draw Coyote under bridge.**) Then Coyote started sweating and grunting like he was doing a hard job.

Rabbit stopped and stared at Coyote. He asked, "Coyote, whatever are you doing?"

Coyote said, "Oh, Rabbit, I am so glad that you came along. I was laying here taking a nap, when I heard the rock above me begin cracking. See that crack there? I jumped up and pressed against the rock as hard as I could. I have been holding this mountain up since early this morning. If I let go, it will come tumbling down. But now my arms are getting so tired. Rabbit, you are strong. Will you hold it up while I go for help?"

Rabbit did not want the mountain to crash down so he stood next to Coyote and started pushing up as hard as he could.

Coyote eased out from under the rock. He said, "Push hard, Rabbit. I think that the crack is getting bigger. I'll go for help. Whatever you do, don't stop pushing."

How long do you think Rabbit stood there pushing up on that mountain? An hour? Longer than that. All afternoon? Longer than that. Rabbit stood there until it got very dark and he got very hungry and thirsty. He yelled for Coyote to come back. But Coyote did not come back.

Finally Rabbit yelled, "Coyote, if you do not come back right now, I am going to let the mountain fall down. *COYOTE!* Look out, I'm letting it go!"

Rabbit let go and ran down the mountain as fast as he could. At the bottom of the mountain sat Coyote, laughing as hard as he could! Coyote didn't even try to run away because he knew angry Rabbit was too tired to chase him.

Rabbit yelled, "Coyote, I am going to get you for this!"

The next night Coyote came upon Rabbit again. Rabbit was taking a drink from the pond under the full moon.

As soon as Coyote saw Rabbit he pounced on him and said, "Rabbit, I am going to eat you this very night."

Rabbit said, "Don't eat me Coyote. See that yellow cheese out there on the pond? Eat that instead. It is much bigger than I am."

(#8 Flip drawing to mug only. Fold bees away at line B. Draw round moon in center of mug.)

Coyote said, "But how can I get that cheese? It is way out there in the middle of the pond."

Rabbit said, "The cheese is big but the pond is little. All you have to do is drink up the pond. Then the cheese will be all yours. Here, I'll help you."

Coyote let Rabbit go and began to drink the pond water. Rabbit lapped noisily at the water with his tongue. But Rabbit only pretended to drink some of the water. Coyote drank and drank. Coyote drank so much water that he became round and wet as a sponge. Still, the big cheese was no closer than it had been before. Do you know what the big cheese really was?

Yes, that's right. It was the moon. But Coyote didn't know that, did he?

Then, out of the corner of his wet eyes, Coyote saw Rabbit running away. Coyote tried to run after him but he was too heavy with water. Rabbit raced up the mountain. There he got a ladder and climbed up to the moon. Then he pulled the ladder up after him. Rabbit left Coyote far below, sitting on the cold ground and howling at Rabbit to come down from the moon.

Did you know that if you look closely at the moon today, you can see Rabbit hiding there? And to this very day, Coyote howls at the moon every night.

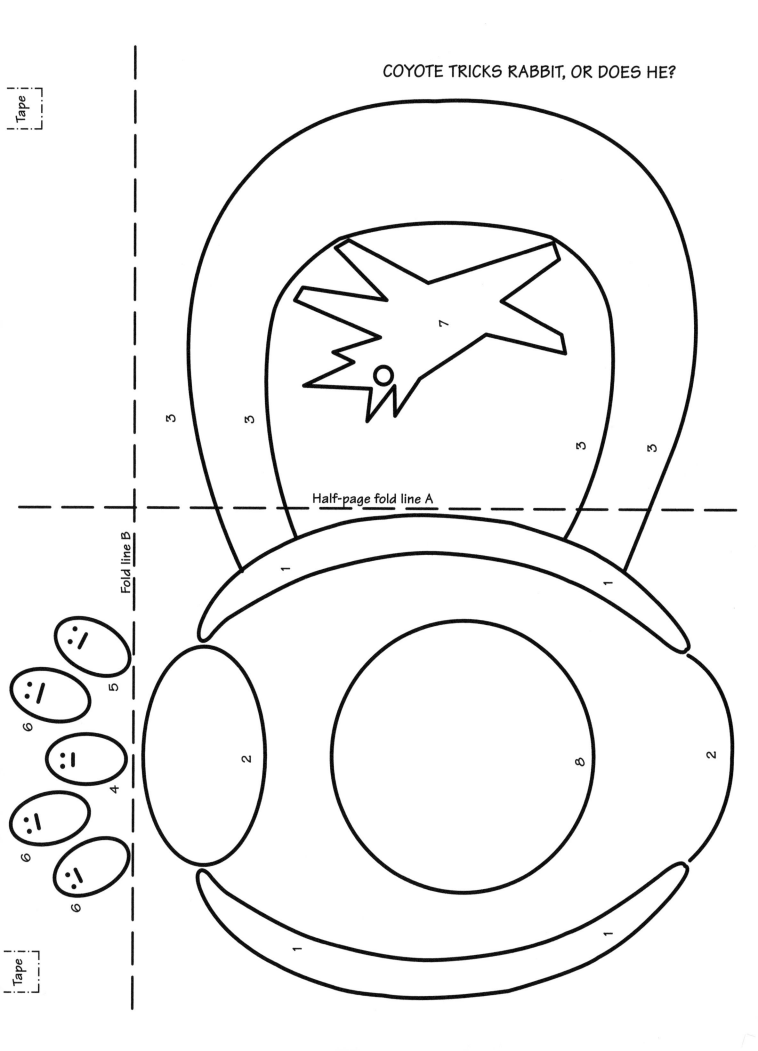

COYOTE TRICKS RABBIT, OR DOES HE?

Tape

Tape

Half-page fold line A

Fold line B

Star Chart

Coyote is a trickster who has been causing trouble or getting into trouble since the beginning of time. In this story, which is based on a Navajo legend, Coyote brings confusion into the lives of the people

In the beginning of the world, the First Woman set out to write all the laws, all the steps, all the rules and all the life plans for everyone. She wanted to make a big chart for all the people of the world. By looking at this chart, everyone would know exactly what to do all of the time.

First, she tried to write the rules in the sand with a big stick. (**Cut 1, wavy lines on the end of paper.**) All went well for several days, but then a strong wind began to blow. It blew the sand around and the words on the chart blurred. The wind had erased the chart that she had so carefully written in the sand.

The First Woman said, "Making the chart in the sand will not work. I must think of something else. Perhaps writing the chart in the water will work." She paddled out to the ocean in her canoe and began to write in the water with her paddle. But as soon as she had written just one or two words, the waves floated over her words and erased them. (**Cut 2, wavy lines at the other end of the paper.**)

The First Woman said, "I need a better place to write my chart, someplace that never changes. How about the sky? But I cannot reach the sky." Just then she stepped on a rock and that gave her an idea.

She said, "I will gather pebbles and throw them into the sky to make the chart." She began to pick up all the pebbles she could find. (**Fold paper on fold lines, making three folds.**) Then she threw one pebble at a time up into the night sky, carefully forming the words with the small stones. When the pebbles landed in the sky, they began to glow and sparkle and shine. Today we call those sparkling pebbles in the sky … stars. (**Cut first star. Put stars in pile where you can reach them.**)

It seemed that each time she threw a pebble into the sky another one appeared in the pile of shiny pebbles at her feet. (**Cut second star as you say this. Put them in the pile.**)

Now you know, all this time, Coyote had been watching from behind a bush. Finally, his curiosity got the better of him and he came out from his hiding place. He asked First Woman, "Why are you throwing all those stones up into the sky?"

She replied, "I am making it easy for all the people who live their lives. I am writing all the rules, laws and steps people should take every day. All they have to do is read from one star to the next. Life will be easy for everyone with this chart. (**Cut third star as you say this. Put stars in pile. Unfold paper and show sky, then refold.**) See how nice and orderly the stars are?"

Coyote asked, "But how can each person see their own life steps in your star chart?"

She answered, "We all look at the same sky but through different eyes. So each person sees a different sky."

Coyote argued, "But writing all the steps and rules for each person will take forever."

First Woman said, "I don't mind how long this chart takes. I know this is a big job to write out all the rules. But the people will need lots of rules and steps for their entire lives."

Coyote said, "This job is taking too long, and besides the people don't need all that much help. Let's get this job done now."

Before the woman could stop him, Coyote gathered up all the pebbles at once and threw them into the sky. **(Pick up and throw all the stars into the air.)**

Now the sky looked like this. **(Quickly cut small diamonds in opposite sides of folded paper. Then unfold and show paper.)**

The First Woman was very unhappy to see all her work undone by Coyote. She said, "Now see what you've done. There are stars scattered all over the sky now. The people will not be able to read the star chart, and they won't know what to do or how to order their lives."

Coyote said, "It will be good for the people to struggle. You were making it too easy for them. Besides the rules are still up there. The people will just have to learn how to look closely and make the best choices they can."

Because of Coyote's trick, the sky is not a star chart with nice orderly rows of stars. It is a confusion of stars every which way.

That is the end of the Navajo legend but not the end of this story.

Because I want to ask you to think back to the time when you were a little kid. Maybe your mom or someone you loved made a little chart for you and stuck it on the refrigerator door. On this chart there were a few things that you were supposed to do—like brush your teeth, take out the trash, or help with the dishes. If you did your job, then your mom put a shiny star on the chart. Little kids are so proud of those stars all lined up in neat rows on their charts. Raise your hand if you ever had a star chart.

Now that you are bigger, you probably don't have a star chart on your refrigerator anymore. But I bet you've done lots of things lately, even just today, to earn a star on your chart. Do you know that you still have a star chart? But it's not on your refrigerator. Do you know where it is? Anytime you want to see it, just go outside and look up into the night sky. When you see all those stars on your chart in the night sky, you will know that each shining star represents a positive thing in your life, past, present and future. **(Hold paper against a white or yellow background.)**

Remember, the night sky that you see is your very own sky, because through your eyes, you see the stars differently than anyone else in the world. And I call this story—Star Chart.

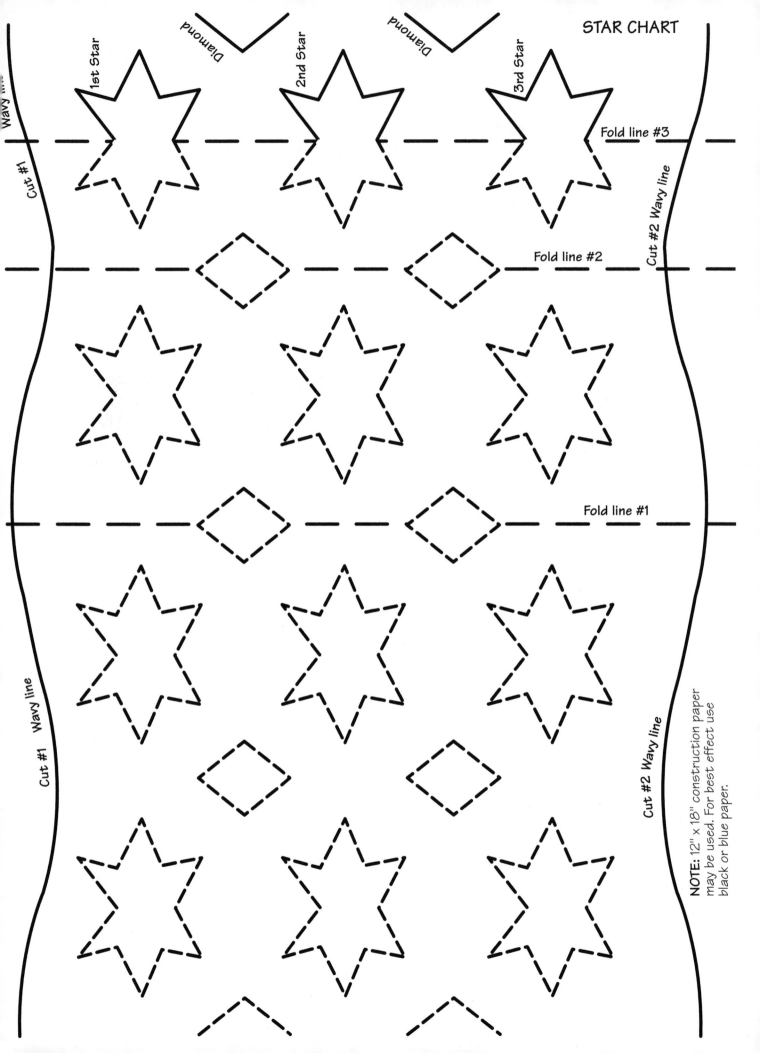

Rabbit Tricks Snake

1 Rabbit is a trickster in many stories. In this story, Rabbit out tricks Snake who has tricked another animal into being his lunch. Variations of this story can be found all over the world.

Far ago, Snake was slithering through the forest looking for his lunch.

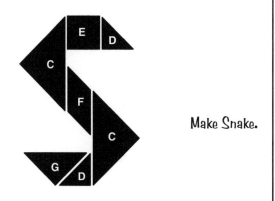

Make Snake.

2 A tree branch fell on him. Snake twisted and turned and squirmed and squiggled every which way, but he could not get free. *(Move snake pieces around to show snake trying to escape.)*

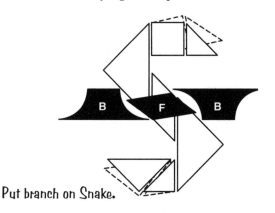

Put branch on Snake.

Finally, Snake gave up and laid still on the ground exhausted.

3 Pretty soon Mouse came scurrying along. Snake called out, "Wait up there, Mouse. What's your big hurry? Stop and chat with me for awhile."

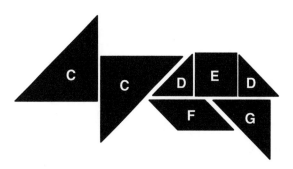

Make Mouse. Use a second set of puzzle pieces so that Snake can remain in the picture.

Mouse replied, "Fox is chasing me. Gotta go."

But then Mouse did stop for a moment and asked, "Why would you want to chat with me, Snake? What you really want to do is eat me."

Then Mouse noticed the big branch laying across Snake's back. He asked, "Hey, Snake, how did that big branch get across your back? You look like you're stuck there."

Snake said, "Mouse, as always, you are so clever. This branch fell on me out of the blue. Mouse, you are stronger than you look. Could you please move this pesky branch off of me?"

"I'm not that strong," Mouse replied. "And besides, if I move this branch off of you, then you'll be free to catch me. At least now I'm safe from you, if not from Fox. Now I really do have to run."

31

4 Right after that Fox came running by.

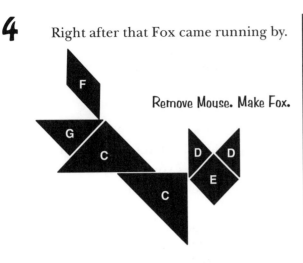

Remove Mouse. Make Fox.

Snake called out, "Wait up there, Fox. What's your big hurry? Stop and chat with me for awhile."

Fox replied, "I'm chasing Mouse. Gotta go."

But then Fox did stop for a moment and asked, "Why would you want to chat with me, Snake? What you really want to do is try to steal my food."

Then Fox noticed the big branch laying across Snake's back. He asked, "Hey, Snake, how did that big branch get across your back? You look like you're stuck there."

Snake said, "Fox, as always, you are so clever. This branch fell on me out of the blue. Fox, you are very strong. Could you please move this pesky branch off of me?"

Fox replied, "Yes, I could move the branch, but then you would probably catch Mouse before I do. Now I have to run."

5 Pretty soon, Bear came lumbering by.

Remove Fox. Make Bear.

Snake called out, "Wait up there, Bear. What's your big hurry? Stop and chat with me for awhile."

Bear replied, "I'm looking for honey. Gotta go."

But then Bear did stop for a moment and inquired, "Why would you want to chat with me, Snake? What you really want to do is try to bite me if I accidentally step on you."

Then Bear noticed the big branch laying across Snake's back. He asked, "Hey, Snake, how did that big branch get across your back? You look like you are stuck there."

Snake said, "Bear, as always, you are so clever. This branch fell on me out of the blue. Bear, you are very strong. Could you please move this pesky branch off of me?"

Bear replied, "Yes, I could move the branch, but then you would probably bite me. Now I have to run."

Snake said in his nicest voice, "Bear, don't go. You haven't stepped on me and so I would have no cause to bite you, now would I? I wouldn't do that to a fellow critter who helps me."

Bear said, "Do you promise, Snake?"

Snake said, "Yes, I promise, Bear."

So Bear lifted the branch off of Snake. Immediately, Snake slithered across the path in front of Bear.

Just then, Mouse came running with Fox close on his heels.

They both stopped when they saw Snake blocking the path, and Bear standing next to him.

Snake said, "What luck! Now I can bite all three of you!"

Bear said, "But you promised not to bite me, Snake."

Snake said, "A snake's gotta do what a snake's gotta do."

6

Snake opened his mouth to bite Bear but just then Rabbit came hopping up. He said, "What is going on here?"

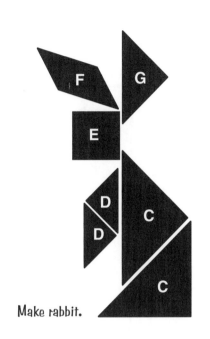

Make rabbit.

Mouse, Fox, Bear and Snake all began to talk at once.

Finally, Rabbit got the whole story out of them.

Rabbit turned to Snake and said, "I'm not quite sure I understand how you ended up under that branch. It doesn't look all that heavy. I bet you could crawl right out from under it if you wanted to."

Snake replied, "No, Rabbit, I tell you that branch was too heavy for me to crawl out from underneath it."

Rabbit argued, "It doesn't look that heavy. I think you're just fooling us Snake."

Snake got angry and yelled, "Are you calling me a liar? That branch is heavy I tell you. Here, there is obviously only one way to prove it. Put the branch on my back, and I will show you that I cannot crawl out from under it because it's too heavy."

Rabbit very calmly asked, "You want me to put the branch back on you Snake?"

"Yes," yelled Snake. "Now!"

7

Rabbit said, "Well, all right. Here goes." He picked up that branch and dropped it on Snake with a thud.

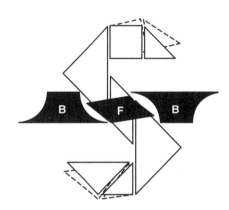

Put branch back on Snake.

Snake squiggled and squirmed and then he said, "See, I told you I couldn't get out from under this branch. Now do you believe me?"

Rabbit said, "Well, I guess I do. Whoever would have thought it?"

Snake said, "Okay, okay. Now just lift the branch off of me again. It is so heavy. I mean *Right Now!*"

Rabbit said, "Oh, no, Snake. You are going to stay right there for awhile."

Then Rabbit added, "Bear, you believed Snake when he said he would not bite you. Have you ever heard the phrase 'Consider the source?' It means you need to think about who says a thing before you believe it. I'm sure that in the future you will carefully consider who and what to believe. Then you can decide what you should do. You need to learn this, Bear."

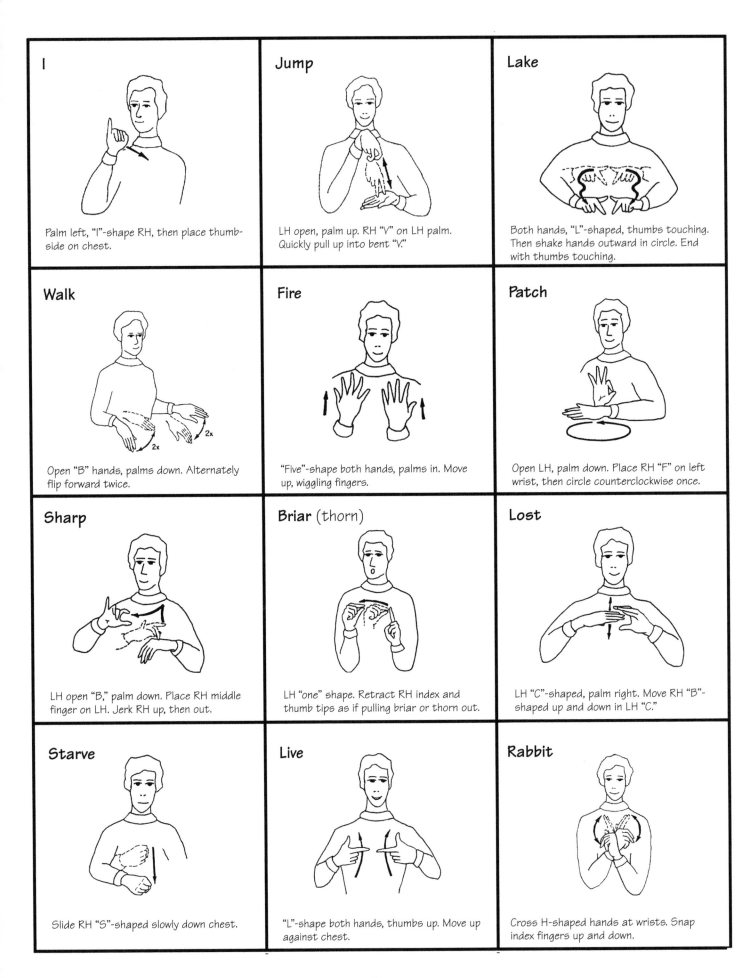

I

Palm left, "I"-shape RH, then place thumb-side on chest.

Jump

LH open, palm up. RH "V" on LH palm. Quickly pull up into bent "V."

Lake

Both hands, "L"-shaped, thumbs touching. Then shake hands outward in circle. End with thumbs touching.

Walk

Open "B" hands, palms down. Alternately flip forward twice.

Fire

"Five"-shape both hands, palms in. Move up, wiggling fingers.

Patch

Open LH, palm down. Place RH "F" on left wrist, then circle counterclockwise once.

Sharp

LH open "B," palm down. Place RH middle finger on LH. Jerk RH up, then out.

Briar (thorn)

LH "one" shape. Retract RH index and thumb tips as if pulling briar or thorn out.

Lost

LH "C"-shaped, palm right. Move RH "B"-shaped up and down in LH "C."

Starve

Slide RH "S"-shaped slowly down chest.

Live

"L"-shape both hands, thumbs up. Move up against chest.

Rabbit

Cross H-shaped hands at wrists. Snap index fingers up and down.

Brer Rabbit Steals Water

Brer Rabbit Steals Water

Brer Rabbit is a trickster in many tales. All the time he is busy figuring out ways to get out of work and get something for nothing. Occasionally, he gets caught. When that happens, Brer Rabbit figures out a way to get out of his punishment. This is a very well-known story about Brer Rabbit.

Far ago there was a great drought in all the land. All the rivers, creeks, and drinking holes that the animals used had dried up. Why, it hadn't rained in such a long time that the animals decided to get together and dig a well. That was such a big job that everyone had to help, even Brer Rabbit.

But Brer Rabbit had never liked to do any work. All the other animals knew this and they said to Brer Rabbit, "If you don't help us dig the well, then you cannot drink from the well."

Brer Rabbit said, "You know that I do not want to help you dig the well. I simply must not get my paws all dirty. Besides, I do not need to drink water from the well. Every morning, I lick the dew drops from the grass. That's enough for water for me."

The other animals did not think that Brer Rabbit was telling the truth. After all, no one had ever seen him licking up the dew drops. They knew that Brer Rabbit had tricked every single one of them at one time or another.

After a lot of hard digging, they finally got the well finished. Then each day all the animals took a turn going to the well for a drink.

But they all thought that Brer Rabbit was secretly stealing water at night from their well. So one night, they gathered up some sticky pine tar from the pine trees. They fashioned a wolf from the sticky tree sap and set it next to the well as if he was guarding it.

Pretty soon Brer Rabbit hopped up to the well to get a nice long drink. He saw the tar wolf sitting there silently. Brer Rabbit was a little scared by this. He called out, "Who's there? What do you want?"

But the tar wolf didn't answer. So Brer Rabbit said, "If you do not answer me, I will hit you."

Of course, the tar wolf did not answer and so Brer Rabbit hit him. Brer Rabbit hit him again and then he kicked that tar wolf. Brer Rabbit's front paws and his back paws stuck fast to the tar wolf. Brer Rabbit was stuck there for the rest of the night.

In the morning when the animals came to drink at the well, they saw Brer Rabbit stuck to the tar wolf, just as they expected.

All the animals had great ideas on how to punish Rabbit for stealing their water.

Bear said, "Let's throw him in the lake. That will punish him."

Brer Rabbit said, "Okay, great. That will be a fine punishment. Go ahead and throw me in the lake."

Brer Rabbit made up a little chant to go with his request. We can use sign language as we are saying (or singing) Brer Rabbit's poem. Here are the signs for **Rabbit, I, jump, lake, walk, fire, patch, sharp, briar**. Can you do these signs with me?

Great! Now here is the first verse of Brer **Rabbit**'s song. You can sing it to the tune of "Happy Birthday!" Brer Rabbit chanted:

*I'll **jump** in the **lake**.*
*I'll **walk** in the **fire**.*
*But, I won't go in the **patch***
*with the **sharp, sharp briar**.*

In the second verse, the signs that we will use are **lost, starve, live,** and you already know **sharp** and **briar.** Here is the second verse of Brer **Rabbit's** song:

> *Cause **I** would get **lost**.*
> *Cause **I** would **starve**.*
> *No, **I** can't live in the **patch***
> *with the **sharp, sharp briar**.*

Fox said, "Well, obviously, Brer **Rabbit** would like being thrown in the lake. So we can't do that. Let's think of something else that we can do to him. I know! Let's light a fire under Rabbit and barbecue him for our breakfast."

Brer Rabbit said, "That will be a fine punishment. Go ahead and barbecue me for breakfast. Just remember…" Brer Rabbit began to sing his little song.

> *I'll **jump** in the **lake**.*
> *I'll **walk** in the **fire**.*
> *But, **I** won't go in the **patch***
> *with the **sharp, sharp briar**.*

> *Cause **I** would get **lost**.*
> *Cause **I** would **starve**.*
> *No, **I** can't live in the **patch***
> *with the **sharp, sharp briar**.*

(Ask the children to say or sing the chant with you. If time permits, ask the children to suggest other animals who want to punish Rabbit. What would each animal do to punish Rabbit? After each punishment is suggested, Rabbit happily agrees with it. Then Rabbit and the children say the chant.)

Turtle said, "Well, obviously, Brer **Rabbit** would like being barbecued for our breakfast. So we can't do that. Let's think of something else that we can do to him. I know! Let's throw him in the briar patch so deep that he can never find his way out."

Brer Rabbit said, "No! No! Not that! Don't throw me in the briar patch. Those thorns— they are so sharp. They would tear me into little pieces! Please, anything but that. No! No!"

The animals had finally thought of something that Brer Rabbit was afraid of! Throwing Brer Rabbit in the briar patch would really punish him for stealing their water.

All the animals grabbed a part of Rabbit and pulled him off the tar wolf. Then they picked Brer Rabbit up in their arms and threw him as far as they could out into the briar patch.

When Brer Rabbit landed in the middle of the briar patch, he called out to his friends,

> *I won't **jump** in the **lake**.*
> *I won't **walk** in the **fire**.*
> *But **I** will go in the **patch***
> *with the **sharp, sharp briar**.*

> *Cause **I** can't get **lost**.*
> *Cause **I** can't **starve**.*
> *Cause **I** live in the **patch***
> *with the **sharp, sharp briar**.*

Brer Rabbit bounded away as fast as he could. He was free again, free to create some other mischief.

Rabbit's Wish

Rabbit is a popular trickster and appears in many tales in many lands. The mischievous and cunning rabbit can be found pulling tricks in West Africa, the Caribbean and the United States. In this variation of the story, rabbit wishes for more—more than what he already has.

Rabbit complained to Earth Spirit. He said, "You have given the elephant a big trunk and you have given the giraffe great height, and you have given the rhinoceros a heavy body, and you have given the leopard spots...."

"Enough!" protested Earth Spirit wearily. "What is it that you want from me, little Rabbit?"

"Well," began Rabbit. "Maybe you could give me wisdom or maybe you could make me bigger?"

"Okay, Rabbit, you can have both of those things," replied Earth Spirit.

"Oh great! Thank you, thank you. Can I have them now? Where are they? Where are they? Let me see them!" cried Rabbit excitedly.

But Earth Spirit said, "Not so fast, Rabbit. I'm not *giving* them to you. You have to earn them."

Rabbit said, "I have to earn what I want? Ohhh... What do I have to do? Will it be easy or hard? I hope it's easy."

And so Earth Spirit told him, "Here is what you must do. Bring me a feather from the Eagle of the Sky. Bring me two scales from Big Fish of the Sea. And..."

Rabbit interrupted, "I cannot do that. That's impossible for me to do. Big Fish and Eagle are bigger than me. They would eat me for lunch. You know that."

Earth Spirit said, "Rabbit, you interrupted me. I was not finished telling you what you must do."

Rabbit replied more slowly and quietly this time, "I'm sorry. You mean there are more than two impossible tasks?"

Earth Spirit answered, "Yes. There is one more thing. Bring me a tooth from Lion of the Jungle. Now go!"

Rabbit hopped off thinking about how he could possibly get all those things. And as he thought, a shadow passed over him. Rabbit looked up. There was Eagle of the Sky and he was swooping down toward Rabbit. Rabbit had to think of something quickly.

He said, "Eagle of the Sky, wait! Don't eat me. I have something to tell you. Did you know that you can make two of me? That way you can have twice as big a lunch."

This was such a strange thing to say that Eagle of the Sky stopped and listened to Rabbit.

Rabbit continued on, "Just take your magic feather and brush it over me two times and then there will be two of me."

Eagle of the Sky said, "I don't have a magic feather. Now prepare to be my lunch."

Rabbit said, "Oh yes, you do have a magic feather. It is right there. Just pull it out and brush it over me two times. "

Rabbit pointed to one of Eagle's wing feathers. **(Cut 1, feather which is Rabbit's foot.)**

Eagle of the Sky pulled out the feather that Rabbit had pointed to. He waved it over Rabbit two times but nothing happened. He said, "Nothing happened. You tricked me. This is not a magic feather. Now prepare to be my lunch."

Rabbit said, "Eagle of the Sky, you are not waving the magic feather correctly. Here, give me the feather and let me do it."

Eagle of the Sky handed Rabbit one of his feathers. Now what do you think Rabbit did with that feather? That's right, he ran away as fast as he could. As he ran he yelled, "Eagle of the Sky, the only thing magic about this feather, is that you gave it to me."

Now Rabbit had a feather from Eagle of the Sky. But he still had to get two scales from Fish of the Sea and a tooth from Lion of the Jungle.

Rabbit walked down to the sea. He played his drum as loudly as he could. He beat his drum as fast as he could. Big Fish of the Sea came up to the water's edge to listen.

Then he asked, "Rabbit, could I please have a turn to play your drum? It looks like so much fun."

Rabbit pretended to consider Big Fish of the Sea's request very seriously. Then he said, "Certainly, I will let you play my drum. It's a magic drum. But first you have to give me two of your scales. Just put them in my hat."

Fish of the Sea said, "That's a lot to ask. But here they are. Now let me have a turn playing your magic drum." He pulled out two scales, a big one and a little one and dropped them into Rabbit's hat. **(Cut 2, large and small semi-circles.)**

As soon as Fish of the Sea had dropped his scales into Rabbit's hat, Rabbit picked up his hat, slapped it on his head and hopped away as fast as he could.

Fish of the Sea yelled after him, "You tricked me. You said I could have a turn playing your magic drum."

Rabbit yelled back, "The only thing magic about this drum is that you gave me two scales for it."

Now Rabbit had a feather from Eagle of the Sky and two scales from Big Fish of the Sea. All he needed was a tooth from Lion of the Jungle.

Rabbit went looking for Lion of the Jungle but Lion found him first. He came up

behind Rabbit with a roar. The next thing Rabbit knew he was in Lion's mouth about to be chewed. Quick as a wink, Rabbit pulled out Eagle's feather and tickled the back of Lion's throat. When Lion opened his mouth to cough, Rabbit stuck his drum on top of one on Lion's smaller teeth. Lion bit down hard on the drum. His tooth broke off. Lion was so surprised that he opened his mouth and Rabbit, the feather, and the tooth fell out. **(Cut 3, Rabbit's ear.)**

Rabbit grabbed Lion's tooth and started running. He ran straight to Earth Spirit and showed all three of the things that Earth Spirit had requested.

Rabbit said, "Now can you give me wisdom and make me bigger? I have brought the things that you asked for."

Earth Spirit said, "Listen to me carefully Rabbit. You figured out how to get a feather from Eagle, two scales from Fish, and a tooth from Lion. This shows that you already have courage. The fact that you did these crazy things shows that you don't have much sense. So I will give you extra large and extra fast feet. The next time that you see an animal bigger than you are, you had better run! Run like the wind!" **(Unfold Rabbit, keeping his ears folded and away from your listeners.)** That's why today rabbits can run like the wind!

Rabbit whined, "Thank you for the extra fast feet. But you said that I could be bigger."

Earth Spirit replied, "You would get into too much trouble if you were any bigger."

Rabbit whined again, "But you promised I could be bigger."

"Very well then," said Earth Spirit, reaching down and pulling on Rabbit's ears. Rabbit felt his ears stretch and stretch. Earth Spirit made Rabbit's ears long—very long indeed. **(Unfold Rabbit ears and show how long they are.)** And that's why today rabbits have extra long ears.

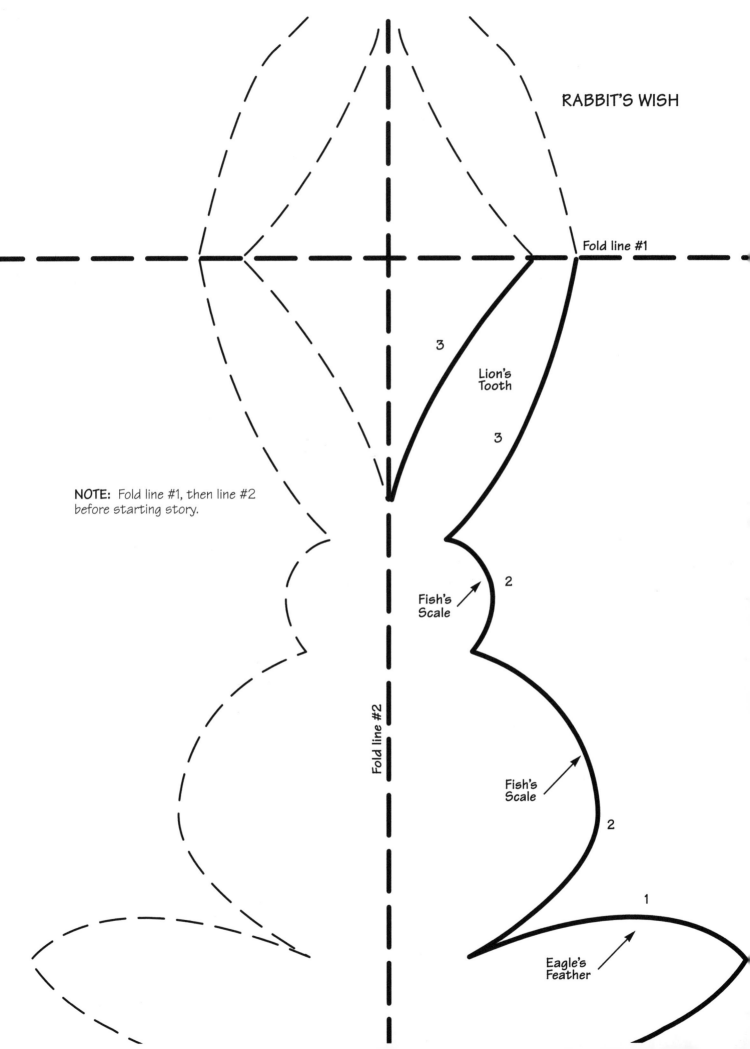

RABBIT'S WISH

Fold line #1

3

Lion's
Tooth

3

NOTE: Fold line #1, then line #2
before starting story.

Fish's
Scale

2

Fold line #2

Fish's
Scale

2

1

Eagle's
Feather

Turtle Tricks Rabbit

Rabbit and Turtle are both tricksters in many tales. In this story, which appears in both Native American and African folktale collections, Turtle pulls a trick on Rabbit.

Every day Rabbit boasted about how fast he could run with his extra big feet. Every day Rabbit criticized Turtle for how slowly he walked. Turtle said that no matter how slowly he walked, he could still beat Rabbit in a race. None of the animals believed Turtle of course, because no one had ever seen Turtle do anything but walk very slowly. But Turtle kept insisting that he could beat Rabbit in a race.

Finally, all the animals agreed that Rabbit and Turtle should have a race and end this silly argument once and for all. They decided to race up and down four hills.

Turtle said to Rabbit, "I'll wear a white feather on my head during the race. That way you will know that it's me." **(Cut 1 to 2 and 3 to 4, feather.)**

Then Turtle talked to three of his turtle friends and they made plans for the race.

Rabbit and a turtle with a white feather started the race at the bottom of the first hill. **(Cut 5 to 6, first hill.)** They started off together but Rabbit was soon far ahead. However, when Rabbit ran over the top of the first hill, he looked ahead and saw a turtle with a white feather crawl over the top of the second hill. **(Cut 7 to 8, second hill.)**

Rabbit began to run faster. But, when he ran over the top of the second hill, he looked ahead and saw a turtle with a white feather crawl over the top of the third hill too. **(Cut 9 to 10, third hill.)**

Now, Rabbit began to run even faster. But, when he ran over the top of the third hill, he looked ahead and saw a turtle with a white feather crawl over the top of the last hill too. **(Cut 11 to 12, last hill.)**

Finally, Rabbit ran as fast as he could, but when he ran over the top of the last hill, he looked down to see turtle with a white feather at the bottom of the hill. Turtle was just going across the finish line. Turtle had won the race!

Rabbit was very upset. He knew that he was faster than Turtle! Nevertheless, Turtle had clearly reached the finish line before Rabbit.

Now, how do you think that Turtle got to the finish line so fast? *(Ask children for their ideas.)*

That's right. There were a total of four turtles in this race. Each one watched for Rabbit to come into sight and made sure Rabbit saw him. When he did, the turtle crawled over the top of the mountain ahead of him. Then the turtle hid himself in the tall grass as Rabbit ran by. Each turtle had a white feather on his head. **(Open up and show all four turtles.)** Rabbit really thought that Turtle had won the race. Rabbit never again boasted or criticized Turtle for being slow. This harmless trick by Turtle taught Rabbit a lesson that he never forgot.

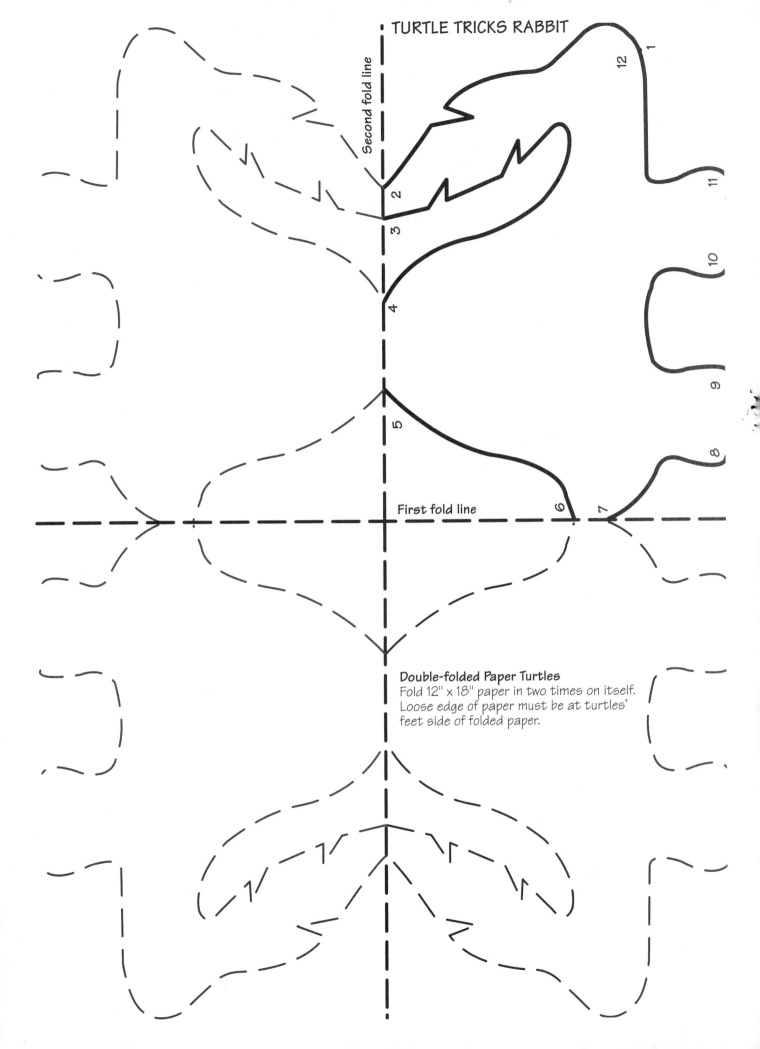

TURTLE TRICKS RABBIT

Second fold line

First fold line

Double-folded Paper Turtles
Fold 12" x 18" paper in two times on itself.
Loose edge of paper must be at turtles'
feet side of folded paper.

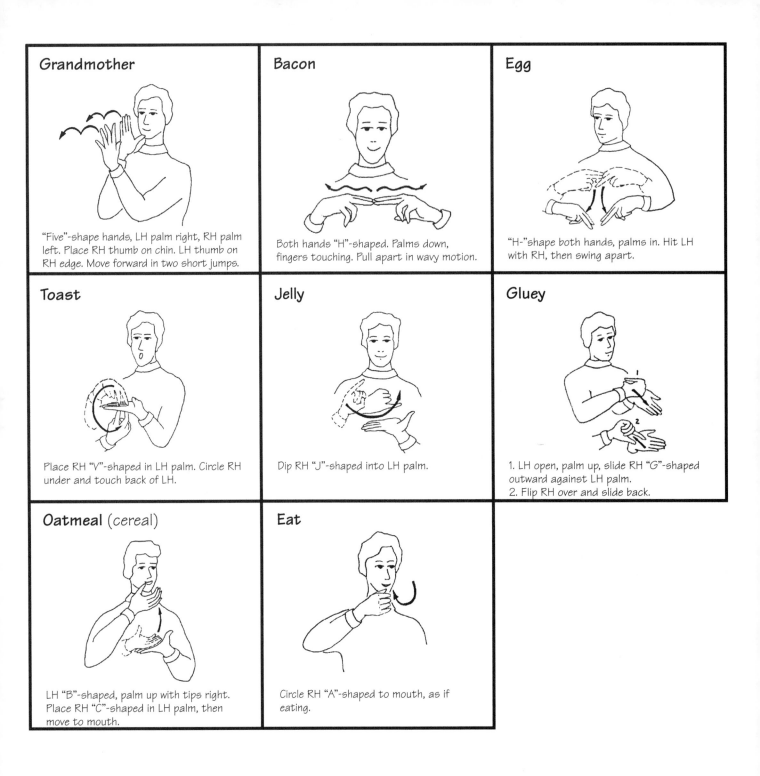

Grandmother

"Five"-shape hands, LH palm right, RH palm left. Place RH thumb on chin. LH thumb on RH edge. Move forward in two short jumps.

Bacon

Both hands "H"-shaped. Palms down, fingers touching. Pull apart in wavy motion.

Egg

"H-"shape both hands, palms in. Hit LH with RH, then swing apart.

Toast

Place RH "V"-shaped in LH palm. Circle RH under and touch back of LH.

Jelly

Dip RH "J"-shaped into LH palm.

Gluey

1. LH open, palm up, slide RH "G"-shaped outward against LH palm.
2. Flip RH over and slide back.

Oatmeal (cereal)

LH "B"-shaped, palm up with tips right. Place RH "C"-shaped in LH palm, then move to mouth.

Eat

Circle RH "A"-shaped to mouth, as if eating.

A Bowl of Cereal

A Bowl of Cereal

Note to the storyteller: This is a true story about Roger, my father. You may wish to tell the story as is, use the name of your father, or simply make the story generic.

When my dad Roger was a little boy, his mother, (who was my grandmother), always made him a big breakfast. It was much too much food for one little boy to eat, especially since he was never hungry first thing in the morning. Yet she expected him to eat it all.

Here are the signs for some important words in our story. Here is the sign for **grandmother, bacon, egg, toast, jelly, gluey, oatmeal, eat.** Let's do these signs together. Then every time in the story that you hear these words, you can do the signs for them.

Every morning, **grandmother** cooked **bacon, eggs, toast** with **jelly** and **gluey oatmeal.** Now Roger liked **bacon, eggs,** and **toast** with **jelly** and he always ate them all up. But he did not like the **oatmeal.** Let me tell you that my **grandmother** was a wonderful cook but she absolutely could not make **oatmeal.** It seemed to always turn out terribly **gluey.** That was why Roger did not like it. But he didn't want his mom to get mad if he complained about her **gluey oatmeal.** So he never told her.

Every morning, my **grandmother** set a big plateful of **bacon, eggs, toast** with **jelly,** and **gluey oatmeal** in front of Roger and said, "Now, Roger, you eat up all of your breakfast before you go to school. I have to leave for work now."

After his mom left, Roger would eat up all his **bacon, eggs,** and **toast** with **jelly.** But the **gluey oatmeal**? What was he to do with it? He didn't want to eat it, but his mother would see

it if he put it in the trash can. (This is in the days before garbage disposals were invented.)

Do you know what Roger did with that **gluey oatmeal** every single morning? He would carefully carry his bowl from the kitchen into the dining room. In the dining room my **grandmother** had a big corner cupboard just filled with all sorts of vases, bowls, candy jars and fancy dishes. She used these special dishes only once a year—and that was at Christmas. On Christmas Day, all of the relatives traveled to her house for a big Christmas dinner.

For days and days my **grandmother** would cook and bake all kinds of wonderful foods. Then on Christmas morning, she would carefully take out all of her vases, bowls, candy jars and fancy dishes. She put all of the food that she had spent so much time cooking into all of the fancy dishes.

But Roger wasn't thinking about Christmas dinner as he went into the dining room. He was only thinking about how to get rid of his **gluey oatmeal.** He opened up the dish cupboard, took out a candy jar and carefully scraped all of the **gluey oatmeal** into the candy jar. Then he put the candy jar back in its place and closed the dish cupboard. Roger did that every morning. After his mom left for work he ate up all of his **bacon, eggs, toast** with **jelly.** He then carefully carried his **gluey oatmeal** to the dining room dish cupboard. He scraped his **gluey oatmeal** into his mom's vases, bowls, candy jars and fancy dishes. When all of those dishes were filled to the brim, he carefully put a thin layer of **gluey oatmeal** in between all of the dinner plates, dessert plates, and saucers. It was a great way to get rid of each day's **oatmeal.**

The days flew by and soon it was Christmas. Roger was so happy to see all of his cousins, aunts and uncles that he completely forgot about several months worth of **gluey oatmeal** packed into every available dish in the dining room cupboard.

Christmas dinner smelled delicious and it was time to sit down to eat. **Grandmother** opened the dining room cupboard and began taking out her fancy dishes. And when she saw that dried up, smelly, moldy oatmeal on every dish, she yelled out, "*Rogerrrr*, come here this instant!"

When Roger heard his mother yelling at him from the dining room, he suddenly remembered about the **oatmeal**. Boy, was he in trouble!

Christmas dinner that year was served and eaten on regular everyday dishes. After Christmas dinner was over, poor Roger couldn't play with his cousins. He had to soak, scrape, wash and dry every single dish that he had put **gluey oatmeal** in. It took him all afternoon!

After that, my **grandmother** continued to fix Roger a big breakfast of **bacon, eggs,** and **toast** with **jelly**. But she never, ever fixed **gluey oatmeal** again. And my dad, even to this very day, never, ever eats **oatmeal.**

At least, that's the way my dad tells it!

The Car Trick

Note to the storyteller: This is a true story about Roger, my father. You may wish to tell the story as is, use the name of your father, or simply make the story generic. You may wish to tell the story as is or omit the introduction.

When my dad was in college, he was a real trickster. Oh, he never did anything that really hurt anyone. He just pulled a lot of funny pranks. Here's one that he is fond of telling to his grandchildren.

One of Roger's favorite professors (teachers) lived so near the college, that he would leave his car in his garage and walk to the building where he taught his classes. **(#1 Draw garage.)**

One Friday evening, the professor invited Roger and some of his friends over to his house. Roger still lived at home, and his mom kept a pretty close eye on him. She told him to have a good time but be home by midnight. **(#2 Draw clock and long minute hand pointing to twelve.)**

Roger walked over to the professor's house. The professor had just bought a new little sports car. He proudly showed it off to the students that evening. While they were all standing around in the garage admiring the new car, Roger happened to notice that the length of the car was exactly the same as the width of the garage. **(#3 Draw bottom of the car. Compare #1 and #3 by pointing to lines 1 and 3.)**

As Roger walked home from the party at midnight, he got an idea. The next night he wanted to go out again with his friends.

His mom again told him to be home by midnight. **(#4 Draw clock with short hour hand pointing to twelve.)**

But on this night, he knew that the professor was out of town for the weekend, even though he had left his garage door up as usual. **(Point to garage door.)** His new little sports car was still in the garage because they had driven his wife's car.

Roger had invited a few of his friends to meet him late that evening in front of the professor's house. He told his friends that they were all going to give their teacher a "surprise."

When the guys finally arrived it was already almost midnight. Roger explained his idea. The friends laughed and then set to work. They gathered round the car and lifted it slightly off the ground. **(#5 Draw back end of car.)** It was so heavy, even for those strong young men, that they had to put it down every few seconds and rest. That car took about three hours to turn sideways in the garage. **(#6 Draw front end of car.)**

Of course, Roger was so involved in directing this mischievous trick that he completely lost all track of the time.

When he finally crept quietly back into his house and got in bed, it was 4:00 a.m. **(#7 Draw short hour hand to 4 o'clock.)**

That morning, Roger came downstairs as usual to breakfast. He did not know if his mom had woken up when he came in so late.

But the first thing she said was, "Roger, I told you to be home by midnight. The very idea of you coming in at 12:20!" **(#8 Draw minute hand pointing to 20 minutes after the hour.)**

Roger was so surprised that he was speechless—at least for a while. And the professor? Well, he was so surprised when he returned home and saw his car cross-wise in his garage that he was speechless—speechless for quite a while! **(#9 Draw garage around car.)**

At least that's the way my father tells it!

THE CAR TRICK

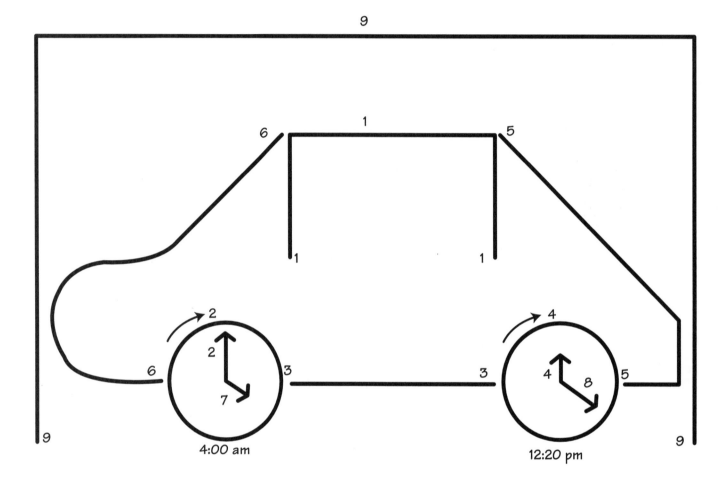

4:00 am

12:20 pm

Charlie's Brand New Car

1 When Roger was twenty years old, he got a job working in a car factory. He worked next to Charlie, a man who was much older than him.

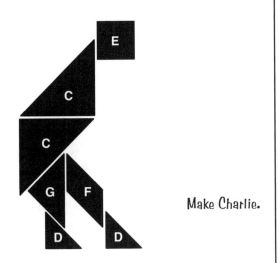

Make Charlie.

Charlie loved his job, his friends at the factory and his family. And he loved cars—especially new ones. Charlie had been saving money for several years to buy a new car. When he felt he had saved up enough money, he spent lots of time looking through car magazines, test driving different cars and talking to all his friends at the factory about what kind of car he should buy.

Charlie asked Roger, "Should I buy a little sports car?"

2 Later Charlie asked, "Maybe I should get a large luxury car?"

Make large car.

Charlie wanted a new car with great looks, great steering, great speed, and great gas mileage. "That's where you get savings, by not having to buy gas very often," Charlie would always say.

Charlie talked every day to Roger and everyone else at the factory about getting a new car. They all got rather tired of hearing Charlie talk about which car had the best looks, fastest speed, best gas mileage, smoothest ride, and the easiest handling.

On the day that Roger had made up his mind to tell Charlie to keep quiet about his new car, Charlie came back from lunch break with a big smile on his face.

"Well, friends, I did it. Today at lunch, I did it. And she's a beauty, gets the best gas mileage in the world," said Charlie.

"Did what, Charlie?" asked Roger, pretending not to know what Charlie was talking about.

"Roger, I bought myself a new car. My new car is so beautiful, and I'm only going to have to buy gas once a week. The gas mileage is that great!" said Charlie.

3

"A beautiful car that gets great gas mileage?" asked Roger.

And that's when Roger, the trickster, got an idea.

Make small car.

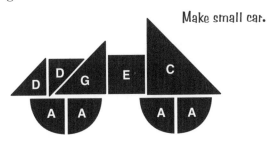

4 Every day at lunch one friend would keep Charlie busy. Roger would go out to the parking lot and quietly put more gas in Charlie's gas tank. Then he would quickly wipe the entire car off with a clean rag, wash the windshield, and scamper off before Charlie could see him.

Make Roger.

Every day Charlie would brag to Roger about his car that never needed gas and even seemed to keep itself clean and shiny.

And every lunch break for two weeks in a row, Roger would sneak out to Charlie's car in the parking lot and quickly put gas in the tank and wipe it clean.

Then one day Roger stopped. He didn't put any more gas in the tank, he didn't wipe it clean and he didn't wash the windshield.

Charlie came to work the next day and didn't brag too much about his new car. A few days later, Charlie was complaining about how the car salesman had tricked him because there was something wrong with his new car.

5 Finally, Charlie took the car back to the car dealership.

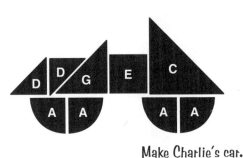

Make Charlie's car.

The mechanic checked everything in the car's engine and he couldn't find anything wrong. The mechanic did think Charlie was a little crazy when Charlie complained that not only did he have to buy gas for his car now, his new car wasn't staying clean by itself like it did for the first two weeks.

Poor Charlie never did figure out Roger's trick—at least that's the way my dad tells it.

The Flagpole and the Tires

Have you ever thought that the assignments your teachers give you don't really have anything to do with the real world?

This is especially true for math. Those math story problems can be downright silly sometimes. At least that's what my dad thought when he was in school.

One day my dad, Roger, complained to his math teacher about how stupid he thought story problems were. "I don't think we should have to do these problems. None of these story problems in this book would ever happen in real life."

So his teacher replied to him, "Okay Roger, you don't like the story problems in the book. Could you make up one of your own? Bring it to class tomorrow. Present your story problem to the class, and we will all try to solve it. If you write a good story problem, I'll give you an extra A for this grading period."

Remember, your story problem has to be one that can happen in real life. But Roger, if the story problem that you come up with isn't any more interesting or practical than the ones in our math book, then I'll give you an extra F. I think that we should let the entire class vote for the A or F. Do you think that's a fair deal?"

Roger agreed, "That's a mighty fine deal and an easy A for me."

Now, my dad was a trickster and a show-off. He wanted to amaze all his friends so he set out to create a super story problem. He told me later that he wanted it to be a story problem that all the kids in his class would remember forever.

He thought about his story problem the rest of the school day and while walking home. **(Cut 1 to 2, inside circle.)**

After getting home, he immediately started out on his afternoon job—delivering newspapers in his neighborhood which was right next to the school.

Roger was thinking about this as he absentmindedly tossed a paper into Mr. Jones's yard. Mr. Jones had a yard full of junk and the newspaper landed behind a pile of old tires. "Rats! Mr. Jones will never see his paper there. I had better go get it." Roger walked into the yard and leaned over the pile of tires to get the newspaper. **(Cut 3 to 4, outside circle.)** But the tires weren't stacked very well and they tumbled all over.

"Mr. Jones needs to stack these tires up better or get rid of them," said Roger.

Just then Mr. Jones came out of his house and called to Roger, "Hey, Roger, what are you doing on those tires? What happened to them? I had them all stacked up!"

"I accidentally threw your paper behind the tires, Mr. Jones. When I leaned over to get it, the tires went every which way. You need to stack them up better, like on a pole or something," said Roger.

Mr. Jones replied, "Heck, I'll just pay you to haul them away for me."

Roger said, "Really? You'd pay me? But where would I put them?"

Mr. Jones chuckled, "Heck, I don't know. Go stack them in someone else's yard. Then it will be their problem."

"Yeah, right," said Roger. He finished his route and returned home thinking about his math story problem.

As soon as she heard the screen door shut, his mother called to him, "Roger, bring in the flag off the flagpole. It looks like it's going to rain."

Roger walked out to the flagpole. **(Cut 5 to 6, side of flagpole.)** On his way back into the house, he got a perfectly wonderful idea. **(Cut 6 to 7, other side of flagpole. Unfold flagpole.)**

The next day, as soon as the bell rang, the math teacher said, "Roger, you look a little tired today. Why, I bet you stayed up all night working on your story problem. So, let's hear it. You promised us an interesting, practical, real-life story problem. Then we'll all vote as a class on your grade. We decided on an A for a great problem and an F for a silly one that's no better than the ones in the math book."

Roger nodded his head and stood up. In a confident voice, he said, "Here's my story problem. It is practical, interesting and could happen in real life. Let's say a person has a flagpole that is twelve-feet tall in his front yard. You want to stack old tires on it all the way to the top. Each tire is nine inches wide. How many tires can you get on your flagpole?" **(Unfold the stacked tires.)**

The class groaned and commented, "Yeah, right! This could never happen in real life. It is definitely not practical! It's rather interesting, but definitely not practical!" The class voted Roger an F. School was dismissed and on the way home everyone, including the teacher, noticed a very tall stack of tires in Roger's front yard.

That evening the entire school was astonished at the picture on the front page of the evening newspaper. The caption stated,

Last night, an unidentified person stacked tires to the top of this flagpole. The flagpole is located in the front yard of a house near the high school. So far, no one has admitted to pulling this prank. The owner of the house was unavailable for comment.

Only then did Roger's math class know that Roger deserved an A+ for his real life math story problem. **(Hold stacked tires over flagpole or thread tires through flagpole.)**

Illustration Note: This story works best with 12" x 18" construction paper.

Pre-cut paper down the center. Fold both "flagpole" and the "stacked tire" pieces of paper lengthwise. These are folds A and B.

Then fold "tire" paper on itself three times before starting story. These are folds C and D. For best effect, use black paper for tires and contrasting paper (yellow, gray, etc.) for flagpole.

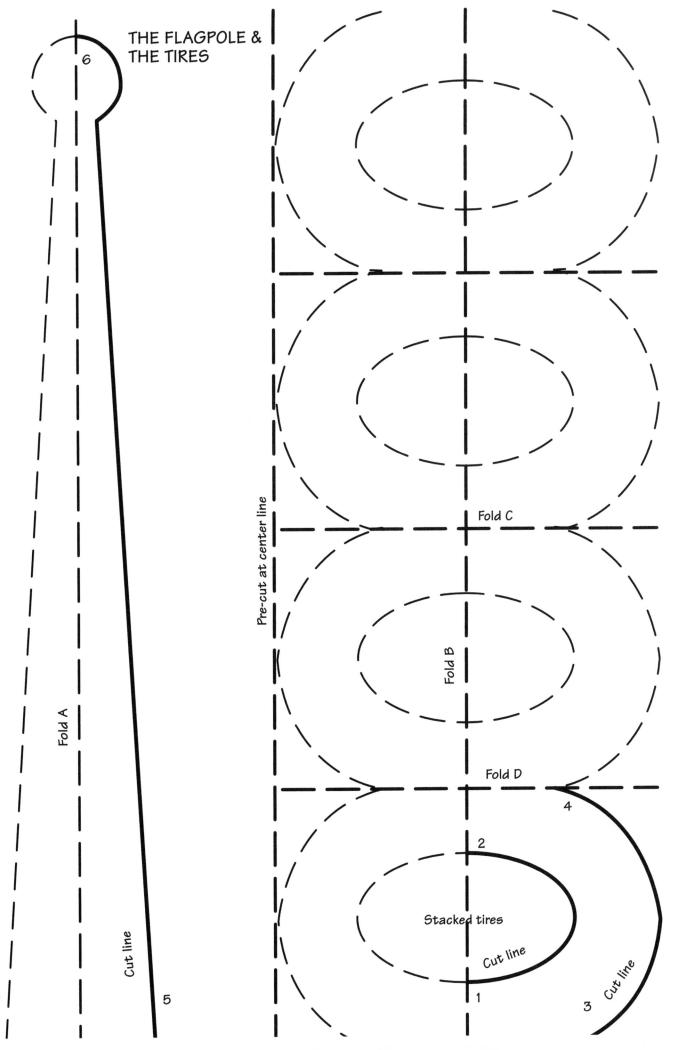

THE FLAGPOLE &
THE TIRES

6

Pre-cut at center line

Fold A

Cut line

7

5

Fold C

Fold B

Fold D

4

2

Stacked tires

Cut line

1

3 Cut line

A Piece of String

Note to the storyteller: This is a true story about Roger, my father. You may wish to tell the story as is, use the name of your father, or simply make the story generic.

My dad has always been a trickster. Here's one of his favorite stories about a trick that a "friend of his" pulled one day. Of course, Dad would never admit that he did this trick himself!

One fine afternoon my dad, Roger, took a big ball of red string from his mom's junk drawer and walked downtown. He was ready to play a trick on someone.

He walked down Main Street looking for some unsuspecting person. The little stores downtown were not very busy. In fact many stores were closed that day. (**#1 Draw building outline and "store."**)

Roger stopped at the first friendly looking person he saw and said, "Excuse me, I'm working on a project for my math class, and I have to measure this building." (**#2 Draw first person.**) I was wondering if you could hold the end of this string for me here at the side of this building. I'm just going to walk around the corner so I can get a good measurement. It might take me a few minutes. I want you to pull on your end of the string every minute or so to let me know you're okay. When I feel your tug, then I'll give an answering tug back to let you know I'm still working on my project. Thank you so much."

Quick as a wink, Roger unrolled his string around the building. On the other side of the building, he asked a second friendly person to hold the other end of his string. (**#3 Draw second person.**)

He said to the second person the exact same thing that he had said to the first person. He said, "Excuse me, I'm working on a project for my math class and I have to measure this building. I was wondering if you could hold the end of this string for me here at the side of this building. (**#4 Draw red string A to B.**) I'm just going to walk around the building so I can measure it. It might take me a few minutes. I want you to pull on your end of the string every five minutes or so to let me know you're okay. When I feel your tug, then I'll give an answering tug back to let you know I'm still working on my project. Thank you so much."

Then Roger walked along the building, dragging his finger along the string as if he were checking on it. As soon as no one was watching, he ducked into the building through the store's front door. (**#5 Draw door and knob.**) He watched for awhile as the two unsuspecting people tugged on the string every few minutes. (**#6 Draw window with Roger's smiling face.**)

Then Roger went home to supper.

And if those two poor unsuspecting souls haven't left yet, why I guess they're still there pulling on the string every few minutes. (**Fold paper together to show 2 people with string.**)

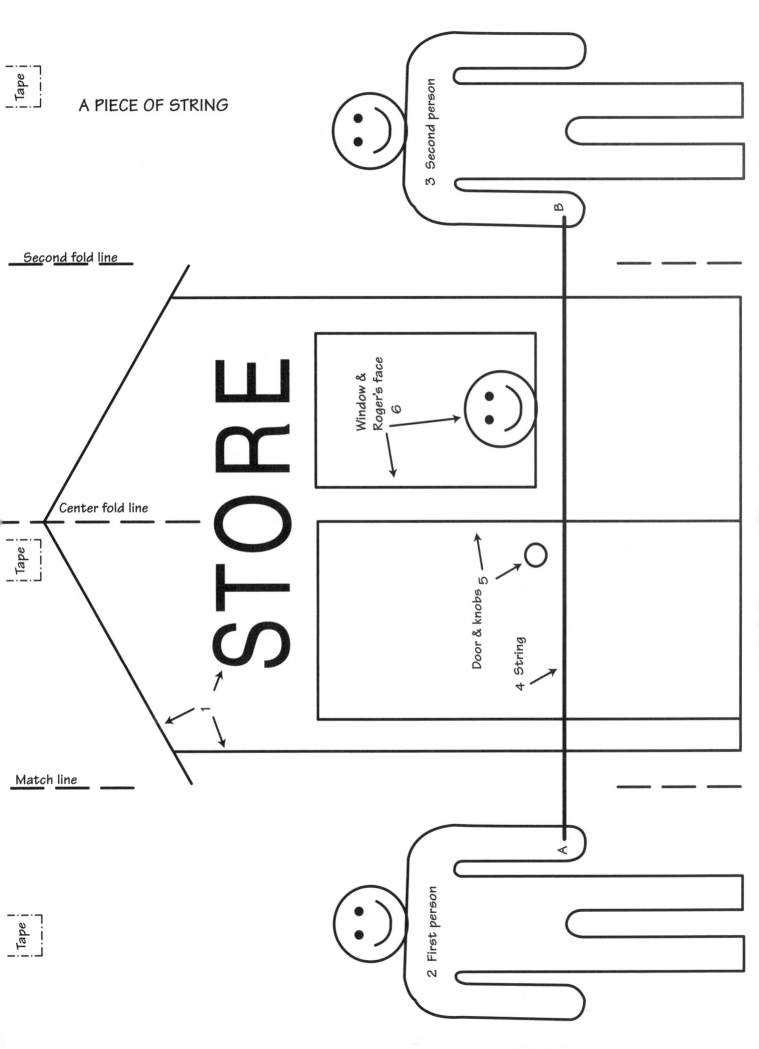

A PIECE OF STRING

Tape

Tape

Tape

Second fold line

Center fold line

Match line

STORE

Window & Roger's face 6

Door & knobs 5

4 String

3 Second person

2 First person

A

B

Raven Steals Light

All along the Pacific Northwest coast Raven is a central figure in many of the stories and trickster tales told by Native Americans. In some of the stories, Raven is greedy and cunning and makes trouble. But in other stories, Raven uses his power to help humans. In this story, Raven sets out to help the people by using his unique magical ability to change his shape at will.

Far ago, Raven flew around the world. (**#1 Draw wing.**) He flew about in the cold, dark world. For back then, the world had no sun or warmth. There was no light anywhere. Raven was sad for himself and for the people because they were all living in darkness.

Raven flew everywhere looking for light. Finally he discovered it, seeping out from the corners of the Sky Chief's lodge. It seemed that Sky Chief had light hidden somewhere in his lodge. Raven flew closer and closer.

Just then, the daughter of the chief came out of the lodge.

She walked down to the edge of the pond carrying a basket. (**#2 Draw circle for pond.**) She knelt down, dipped her round woven basket into the water, and took a drink. (**#3 Draw second circle for basket.**) Then she dipped her basket in the water a second time.

Quickly, Raven changed himself into a pine needle. (**#4 Draw pine needle.**) He floated down and landed in the water. As the princess drank the second time, she swallowed the pine needle.

After a while, the princess gave birth to a baby boy with shiny black hair and sparkling dark eyes. The baby was really Raven. Everyone, especially Sky Chief, loved the hand-some baby boy. (**#5 Draw eyes.**) Sky Chief made his baby grandson rattles and other toys.

Raven was a happy baby. He crawled around and explored everywhere. His mother, the princess, and his grandfather, the Sky Chief, were very indulgent. They let him play with everything that he wanted. They let him play with everything that is, except three boxes hidden high up on a shelf. (**#6 Draw three boxes.**)

Then Raven knew that the light must be hidden in those three boxes. So Raven began to cry and point to the smallest box. He cried and cried. He cried so hard that finally Sky Chief reached up on the shelf and handed down to Raven the smallest box. Raven stopped crying.

Sky Chief said, "Look at the box, my precious grandson, but do not take the lid off." Raven pretended not to hear and took the lid off. Immediately tiny sparkles of light flew out of the box and up through the smoke hole of the lodge. (**#7 Draw smoke hole.**) They landed in the sky. When the people saw the lights, they were happy. Sky Chief was sad that his stars had flown out of the box, but Raven climbed up on his lap and hugged him tightly.

Not long after that, Raven began to cry again and pointed to the second box. He cried and cried. He cried so hard that finally Sky Chief reached up on the shelf and handed the second box down to Raven. Raven stopped crying.

Sky Chief said, "Look at the box, my precious grandson, but do not take the lid off." Again, Raven pretended not to hear and took the lid off. Immediately a small ball of light bounced out of the box. (**#8 Draw ball.**) Raven pretended it was a toy. He rolled it here. (#9 **Draw wing.**) He rolled it there. (#10 **Draw another wing.**) Then, when no one was looking, he threw it up through the smoke hole of the lodge.

The moon landed in the sky. When the people saw the moon they were very happy! Sky Chief was sad that his moon was gone from the box, but Raven climbed up on his lap and hugged him tightly.

Not long after that, Raven began to cry again and point to the third box. He cried and cried. He cried so hard that finally Sky Chief reached up on shelf and handed the third box down to Raven. Raven stopped crying.

Sky Chief said, "Look at the box, my precious grandson, but do not take the lid off." Raven pretended not to hear and took the lid off. Immediately a larger ball of light bounced out of the box. (#11 **Draw another eye.**) Raven pretended it was a ball.

He rolled it here. He rolled it there. (#12 **Draw figure eight for nostrils.**) But always Sky Chief watched Raven play with the ball and then put it safely back into the box.

So, one day, when no one was looking, Raven changed himself back into a bird. He grabbed the box with his claws and flew toward the smoke hole to escape with the box. But in that instant, Sky Chief realized that he had been tricked.

Sky Chief cast a spell on the smoke hole to close it shut.

But Raven was already half-way through the smoke hole. He managed to squeeze through the hole with the box. But not before his beautiful feathers became stained with soot, turning him completely black.

Raven flew as high in the sky as he could. Then he opened the box with his beak. (#13 **Draw beak.**)

That is how Raven gave the light of the stars, the moon and the sun to the people. That is also how Raven became as black as soot. This is why today the people always feed Raven, to thank him for bringing the light. (#14 **Draw mouth.**)

This story of Raven often appears on totem poles. Totem poles record family and tribal history, and Raven is an important part of Native American history. The top figure is the Thunderbird figure. The Thunderbird represents the Klallam, a Native American tribe. The middle drawing represents Raven who brought light to the people. The bottom figure represents Sky Chief.

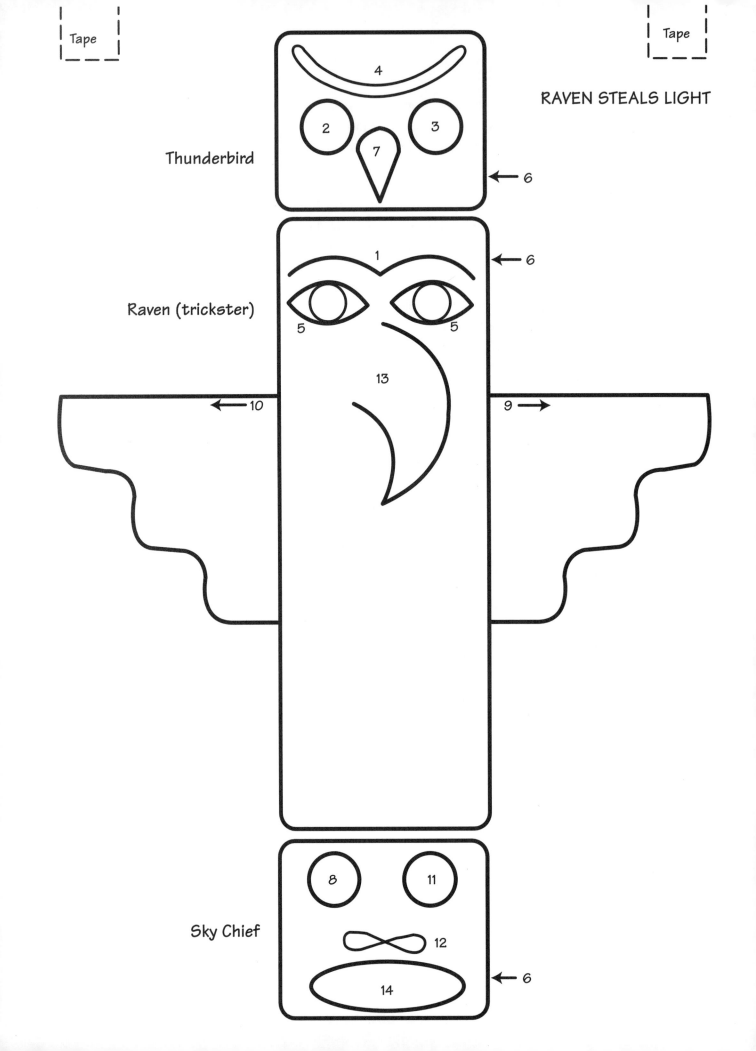

Tape

Tape

RAVEN STEALS LIGHT

Thunderbird

4

2   3

7

← 6

Raven (trickster)

1

← 6

5   5

13

← 10

9 →

Sky Chief

8   11

12

← 6

14

A Lazy Farmer

People tell trickster tales in every land and in every culture. A trickster can take the form of a turtle, rabbit, bird, coyote, or spider. In many stories, the trickster tries to get someone else to do his work for him. This is very much like we are as human beings. Occasionally, the trickster is a person. In this story, a farmer is the trickster.

Far ago there was a poor farmer who loved spring. He loved spring's warm breezes and wonderful sunshine. His favorite thing to do was to sit on his porch in his rocking chair, listening to his radio, drinking a cold soda and enjoying spring.

One fine spring day, the rich landowner from whom the farmer rented his land walked by. The landowner said, "Farmer, you should be out in my fields, getting them smooth and ready for the spring planting. What are you doing?"

The farmer answered from his porch, "I am rocking in my rocking chair, listening to my radio, drinking my cold soda and enjoying spring." (**#1 Draw house with porch.**)

The landowner replied, "All my other farmers are out in my fields, getting them smooth and ready to plant. You should be out there also." (**#2 Draw outline of field.**)

"Maybe tomorrow," replied the farmer.

The next day the rich landowner walked by and saw the farmer on his porch again. He said, "Farmer, you should be out in my fields, getting them smooth and ready for the spring planting. What are you doing?"

The farmer answered from his porch, "I am rocking in my rocking chair, listening to my radio, drinking my cold soda and enjoying spring."

The landowner replied, "All my other farmers are out in my fields, getting them smooth and ready to plant. You should be out there also." (**#3 Draw outline of field.**)

"Maybe tomorrow," replied the farmer.

The day after that the rich landowner walked by and saw the farmer on his porch again. He said, "Farmer, you should be out in my fields, getting them smooth and ready for the spring planting. What are you doing?" (**#4 Draw outline of field.**)

The farmer answered from his porch, "I am rocking in my rocking chair, listening to my radio, drinking my cold soda and enjoying spring."

The landowner replied, "All my other farmers are out in my fields, getting them smooth and ready to plant. You should be out there also."

"Maybe tomorrow," replied the farmer.

On the fourth day the rich landowner again walked by, but this time he said, "Farmer, everyone else has been working in my fields all this week. If you do not have your field smoothed and ready for planting on Monday, I am going to rent your field to someone else. Remember—Monday—have your field smooth and ready for planting."

The next day the farmer got off of his porch long enough to walk down the rocky road to town. (**#5 Draw line across paper.**)

He carried a big cardboard sign. He nailed the sign to the side of a building where everyone would see it. (**#6 Draw square sign.**)

Then the farmer walked back home along the gravel road. (**#7 Draw line and dots for gravel.**)

The very next day, Sunday, all the townspeople walked down the road to the farmer's house. When they arrived, there was the farmer. What do you think he was doing? Yes, that's right. He was sitting on the front porch, rocking in his rocking chair, listening to his radio, drinking his cold soda and enjoying spring.

But this time, he was holding a long bamboo pole in his hand. He said, "I see you all read my sign. Now you have come to see me climb to heaven on a bamboo pole. Well, let's get started."

The farmer led all of the people of the town out into his field. He said, "I learned the trick of climbing to heaven from a wise man. He told me to place the pole in all four corners of the field, in the middle of the field and all points in-between. Then I would be able to climb to heaven."

The farmer walked to the far corner of his field. All the people followed him. He stuck the pole firmly in the ground. Then he slowly began climbing the pole. But the pole bent under his weight and the farmer had to jump off before he crashed to the ground. All the people laughed. They had doubts all along that the farmer could climb up to heaven on a pole. But they wanted to be there just in case he really did it.

The farmer said, "Don't laugh just yet. Let me remind you that the wise man told me to try all four corners of the field, the middle and all points in-between."

All day long the people followed him from far corner to far corner, the middle of the field and all points in-between. Each time, the farmer planted the pole firmly in the ground. Each time, when he got about halfway up the pole, he had to jump off before he crashed to the ground.

Finally, the people began to get tired of following the farmer all over his field. It began to get dark and one by one they walked back to town.

The next morning, the landowner walked by. He was very angry and yelled, "Farmer, every day last week I told you to get out in my fields, and get them smooth and ready for the spring planting. I gave you until Monday, but you didn't do it. Today is Monday, and what are you doing?"

The farmer answered from his porch, "I am rocking in my rocking chair, listening to my radio, drinking my cold soda and enjoying spring."

The rich landowner was so angry that he did not bother to look at his field. He yelled, "You did not get my field smoothed. Get off my land."

The farmer answered calmly, "See for yourself. The field is smooth and ready for planting. I will do the planting today. I love to plant. I just don't like to spend time breaking up all those clods and clumps of dirt."

The surprised landowner yelled, "When did you do all this work? How did you do this work?"

The farmer answered, "I did it yesterday, with a little help from my friends down the road and my bamboo pole." (**Fold paper to match line to show smooth field and bamboo pole.**)

Teller's Note: For a very effective yet simple method, take one piece of paper and fold it in half. When you come to the point in the story when the farmer walks out onto the field with his friends, wrinkle up half the paper. Tell your listeners that this represents the rough field.

At the end of the story, the field is smooth. At this point, show the smooth half of the paper. Discuss the difference and how this happened.

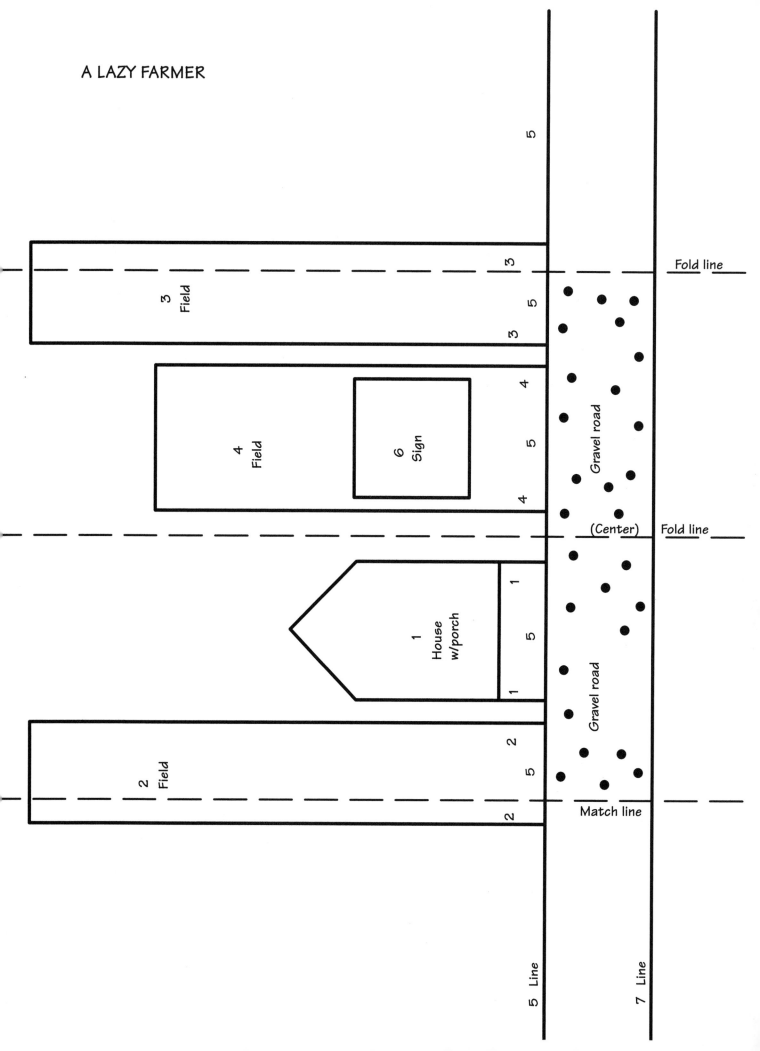

The Trojan Horse

1 The fall and destruction of the mighty city of Troy is told in an epic poem called the *Aeneid.* The poem was written by the Roman poet, Virgil. Troy was an ancient city in what is now Turkey. This story is one of the most famous trickster tales in the world.

Far ago, in the city of Sparta, in the country of Greece, a young man and a young woman fell in love. The young woman's name was Helen, and many people thought that she was the most beautiful woman in the world.

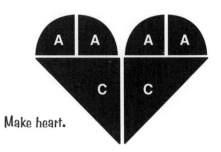

Make heart.

But it was definitely not wonderful in this case. In fact, when Helen and Paris fell in love with each other, it started a war that lasted over ten years.

What was the problem? The problem was that Helen was already married to the king of Sparta, King Menelaus.

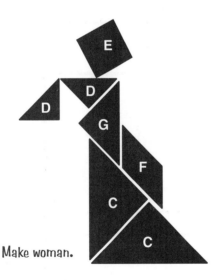

Make woman.

2 The young man that she fell in love with was called Paris. Paris was visiting in the city of Sparta when he met Helen. You would think that a man and woman falling in love with each other was a wonderful thing.

3 When King Menelaus found out that his beautiful wife Helen had run away to the city of Troy with Paris, he was furious!

Make king's head with crown.

King Menelaus was so furious that he and his brother, Agememnon, organized a great army of Greek soldiers.

60

4 They sailed to Troy after Helen.

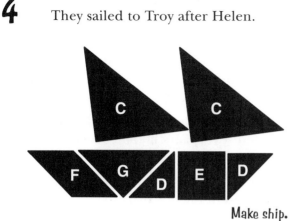

Make ship.

When they arrived, the Greek soldiers camped outside the city walls of Troy. The soldiers attacked the city again and again, but the great strong walls around the city kept Troy safe.

Both sides had powerful, well-trained soldiers. Both sides desperately wanted to win. Both sides fought bravely week after week, month after month, and year after year, but neither side could win.

5 The Greek army laid siege to (or camped outside) the city for ten years! But they couldn't get past the city walls.

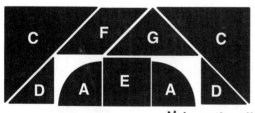

Make castle wall.

At the end of ten years, Odysseus ordered some of his soldiers to build a giant wooden horse. Odysseus and several of his best soldiers hid inside the wooden statue.

The rest of the Greek soldiers packed up their shields, swords, and all the rest of their camp. They carried everything down to the seashore and loaded it into their waiting ships. Then all the ships sailed away.

6 The people of the city of Troy watched all this in total amazement. Could it be that after ten long years, the Greek soldiers had just given up? For the first time in ten years they opened the gate to their walled city and came out.

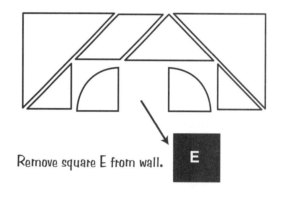

Remove square E from wall.

7 They walked about. As they walked, they discovered a tall wooden statue. On the beach was the biggest wooden horse they had ever seen. They walked slowly around it. Everyone was talking about the horse.

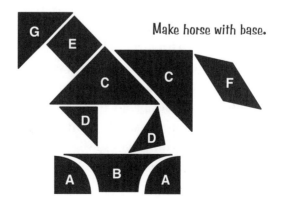

Make horse with base.

8 The high priest, Laocoon was shouting. He was saying something about never trusting the Greeks. He was certain that this must be a trick. He took a spear from a guard and threw it at the horse's belly. The spear bounced off the wood, making a strange hollow sound. But no one paid attention to it.

Then out from under the platform that the horse was built on rolled a small man. His hands were tied behind him.

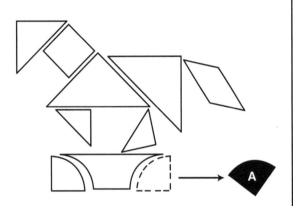

Pull "A" piece out from under horse base.

Immediately, the guards pointed their spears at him.

He said, "Please don't hurt me. My name is Sinon. I was a prisoner of the terrible Greek soldiers. I escaped and hid under their gift to Athena."

The Trojans asked him, "Where did this horse come from? What is it for? Whose side are you on?"

Sinon answered, "The Greeks built this great horse to the war goddess Athena. It was a gift to her so she would give the Greek soldiers her protection. The Greeks were afraid that you would want this beautiful horse for yourselves so they made the horse too big and too tall to fit through your city gates."

What Sinon did not explain was why the Greeks had sailed away, especially after building such a beautiful horse. But the Trojans didn't think about that. What they were most concerned with was that the Greeks didn't want the Trojans to have their horse. Because of this, the Trojans wanted it very much. The Trojans began pulling at the horse. They wanted to roll him into the city. Such a fine horse surely belonged in the city of Troy.

9 They soon saw that the city's gates were indeed too small for the horse to fit through. So the people began tearing down the gates of the city.

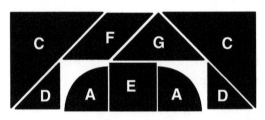

Remake wall. Remove pieces "A," "E," "F" and "G" from the center.

10 Laocoon begged the people to stop and think about what they were doing. They ignored him and went on destroying their city walls. Then the strangest thing happened. Two snakes came out of the sea and slithered straight towards Laocoon and his two sons.

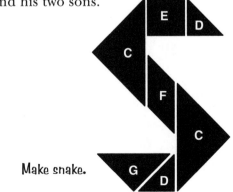

Make snake.

They wrapped themselves around Laocoon and his sons and killed all three of them instantly.

Of course, all of the people of Troy took this as a sign that Laocoon was wrong, and they should indeed pull the wooden horse into their city. As they pulled on the horse, they heard a strange sound, like the clanking of metal.

11

As they pulled the horse into the city, everyone began dancing and singing so loudly that the metal clanking could no longer be heard. The people danced and sang around the wooden horse all day long.

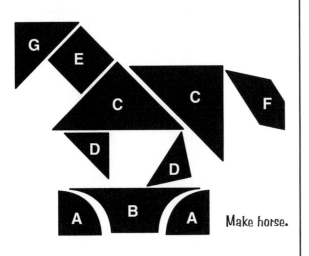

Make horse.

Finally, night came and all the Trojans fell into a deep sleep. They were tired from the day's activities of destroying the city gates, rolling the heavy horse into the city and then dancing and singing until night fall.

When the night was at is blackest, Sinon quietly climbed one of the city's walls. He stood looking out to sea. He was watching for a signal. As soon as he saw a small fire, he knew that the Greek ships had returned. The Greek soldiers had spent the day hiding on a nearby island. Sinon quickly climbed down from the wall. He ran over to the wooden horse and opened a small, cleverly concealed trapdoor.

The soldiers who had been hiding in the wooden horse all day, squeezed out, stretching their legs, and happily breathing the fresh air.

The Greek soldiers captured the sleeping Trojan guards. Then they ran around setting fire to the city. The Trojans put up a brave fight. But since they had been completely surprised by the Greeks' attack, they had no time to get ready. They could not find their weapons to defend themselves and did not have the protection of the walls of their city.

By morning, the magnificent city of Troy lay completely in ruins. The wooden horse still stood in the middle of the town, completely forgotten. Paris and many other noble soldiers had been killed.

12

King Menelaus sailed back to Greece with his soldiers. On board their ship was the beautiful Helen.

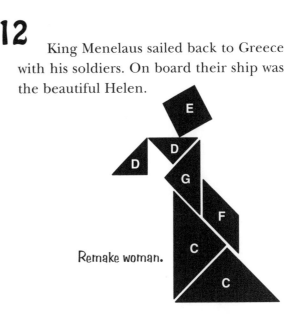

Remake woman.

Since then, many, many stories and poems have been written about Helen, the wooden Trojan horse, and the amazing trick that brought about the fall of the city of Troy.

Paper-Cutting Directions

What is Paper-Cutting?

Cutting the "answer" to a story out of a folded piece of paper is a unique way to tell a story, and it yields an unusual surprise for the listeners. It is also a great way for children to learn to tell stories. The stories are short, easy to tell and deceptively simple.

As you tell these stories, you will be cutting an object out of a folded piece of construction paper. At the end of the story, the object is completely cut out and unfolded. The paper-cut object is an integral part of the story.

After you tell a few of these stories, your students will soon be telling their own paper-cutting tales both at home and at school. Some children will bring stories to school that they have made up at home; this generates enthusiasm in other children to do the same thing.

Why combine storytelling and Paper-Cutting?

Telling a story while cutting a piece of paper is a great way to completely capture your listeners' interest.

Watching the object emerge from the paper helps both the storyteller and the listeners remember the steps of the story. The cutting lines are related to the plot, and the object created is important to the outcome of your story.

Another plus: When speaking in front of a group, most people feel more confident if they have something to do with their hands; the paper and scissors fulfill this need.

Most children love to cut and spend lots of time at it. After listening to a paper-cutting story involving a simple object, children will often take their own ideas and turn them into a story.

Do you need to be an artist or seasoned storyteller?

No! All you need to do is trace. These patterns are designed to be used with any size and color of paper. You do not have to cut freehand; just trace your cutting lines lightly before telling the story.

How do you get started telling Paper-Cutting stories?

1. First place a piece of white paper over the pattern in the book. With a pencil, trace cutting lines lightly. Fold where indicated. If you are using white paper to tell your story, you are ready to go. If you want to transfer the cutting lines to colored paper, then cut out your white pattern, place it on the colored paper and trace around it.

2. Practice telling your story while cutting so that it becomes natural to talk and cut at the same time. Cutting steps are related to the story. As the character goes somewhere or does something, you cut a new line. Becoming familiar with the story and the cutting allows you to present the story easily and develop a natural rapport with your listeners. When you are not cutting, just hold the paper and scissors naturally or put them down if you want to gesture while talking.

If you forget what comes next or get stuck in a story, ask the youngsters to repeat what's happened thus far (giving you time to think) or suggest what could come next.

3. Retell the story at least once. Retelling the story gives the listener a second chance to enjoy it as well as to learn the story and the cutting steps. Stories can and should be changed by each storyteller, and a story will be a little bit different each time it is told.

4. There are countless variations of paper-cutting. The paper can be folded several times as in "Turtle Tricks Rabbit." You can cut out two different objects as in "The Flagpole and the Tires." You and your students will surprise yourselves at how creative you can be with this paper-cutting concept.

How can you and your students create original Paper-Cutting stories?

1. Decide on a story to tell. Then choose something to paper-cut that is an integral part of the story. Or first choose an object to cut, then find or create a story involving that object. Objects should be symmetrical. "How to Draw" books (available in most libraries) are a great resource for ideas.

2. Students should prefold their paper and draw one half of their object against the folded side lightly with a pencil. Students can make notes, outline their story or even write out their entire story on this paper. Remind them to relate their cutting steps to their story line. As their character goes places or does things, they can make their next cut.

3. This is a great time to teach story elements. Every story needs the following: an introduction, characters, location or setting, action or plot, and resolution or a good ending

4. Expect a wide range of cut-outs and stories. Students' stories might even be remarkably similar to one that you have just told. This is fine and quite a compliment to you. You might need to encourage a reluctant child who "just can't think of anything." Help him draw a picture to cut out from one printed on his shirt, his notebook or hung on a school bulletin board. Get the child started by asking questions such as, "What else does this outline of a snowman make you think of? Does it look like a path? Are some kids walking down this path when they get lost?" *(Indicate outline of snowman.)*

5. Have scissors and several sheets of paper ready for each student. Encourage them to practice telling their story to themselves first and then to a friend. Students may prefer to work together— one partner cuts while the other tells the story.

6. After practicing several times, your storytellers will be ready to present their story to the rest of the group. After their presentation, you might want to present each child with a "Storytelling Certificate" or another story told by you.

Mystery-Fold Directions

What is Mystery-Fold?

Drawing and folding the "answer" to a story out of a piece of paper is a unique way to tell a story, and it yields an unusual surprise for the listener. It is also a great way for children to learn to tell stories.

As you tell these stories, you will be drawing on both the left and right sides of the paper. The drawing lines are related to the plot. At the end of the story, the object is completely drawn. During the last sentence of the story, you fold the paper together to reveal the "answer." After you tell a few Mystery-Fold stories, your students will be telling and folding their own tales.

Why combine storytelling and drawing?

Telling a story while drawing a picture is a great way to completely capture your listener's interest. This is an unusual approach to storytelling, and, because you fold your picture together at the end of the story —Wow! You've got a memorable story!

Most children love to draw and spend lots of time at it. After listening to a Mystery-Fold story, children will often take their own drawings or doodles and turn them into a story.

Do you need to be an artist or seasoned storyteller?

No! All you need to do is trace! The patterns are designed to be used with any size paper.

How do you get started telling Mystery-Fold stories?

1. Drawing steps are related to the story. As the character goes somewhere or does something, you add a new line to your picture.

2. First place a piece of white paper over the pattern in the book. With a pencil, trace all drawing lines very lightly. (Later on, you might let your listeners in on this secret.) Note where you will place the tape.

3. Practice telling your story while drawing so that it becomes natural to talk and draw at the same time. Becoming familiar with the story and the drawing allows you to present the story easily and develop a natural rapport with your listeners.

If you forget what comes next or get stuck in a story, ask the listeners to repeat what's happened thus far (giving you time to think) or suggest what could come next.

After hearing a few stories, children will begin to try to figure out the object you are drawing before you fold the drawing together. You will know by a child's facial expression when he or she knows what it is that you are drawing. If you notice a listener just bursting to "spill" the answer, recognize him or her quietly with an aside such as "Shhh…it's a secret."

4. When you are storytelling with a large group, you will want to tape the drawing paper to a wall or chalkboard. You can enlarge the picture with an opaque projector to make it more easily seen. Drawing on chart paper also works well. Use the lines to help you keep the two halves lined up properly. If you have just a few listeners, everyone could sit around a table.

5. Retell the story at least once. Retelling the story gives the listener a second chance to enjoy it as well as to learn the story and the drawing steps. Stories can and should be changed by each storyteller, and a story will be a little different each time it is told.

How can you and your listeners create your own Mystery-Fold stories?

1. Decide on a story to tell, then choose something to draw and fold that is an integral part of the story. Or choose an object to draw, then find or write a story involving that object. "How to Draw" books (available in most libraries) are great resources for ideas.

2. A basic Mystery-Fold is done by folding the paper in half across the width of the paper, then folding it in half again. Make this fold parallel to the first, which will divide that paper equally into four long rectangular sections. Return to the first fold, and fold the end rectangular section back onto the adjacent one. Now only the two end sections are visible; the middle two sections are not.

3. Prefold your paper and draw lines lightly with a pencil. During the telling of your story, relate

the drawing steps to the storyline. For example, as a character goes places or does things, add new lines to the picture.

4. This is a great time to teach story elements. Every story needs the following:

    a. an introduction
    b. characters
    c. location or setting
    d. action or plot
    e. resolution or good ending

5. Drawings do not have to be symmetrical. You can take any simple drawing, divide it in half, and draw half the picture on one side of the page and the other half on the other side of the page. You can divide your drawing horizontally or vertically.

    Remember, the picture is drawn on the end sections only. If you feel the picture will be easily guessed while you are telling the story, draw your picture upside down or sideways.

6. If you are drawing a picture that is symmetrical, the second character can repeat what the first character said. Both the storylines and the drawing lines are repeated and symmetrical. This makes it easy for a child to remember.

7. Expect a wide range of quality in the drawings and stories created by your listeners. Their stories might even be remarkably similar to one that you have just told. This is great—and quite a compliment to you!

8. Plan to have several sheets of paper for each student. Encourage them to tell their story to themselves first and then to a friend. Students may prefer to work together in writing and telling their story. When they tell their story to you, you can help them "work out the bugs."

9. After practicing several times, your storytellers will be ready to present to the rest of the class. After their presentation, you might want to reward each child with a "Storyteller's Certificate" or a story told by you.

Sign Language Directions

Why sign language?

Sign language is as beautiful as a ballet. Add it to a good tale, and you've got a winning combination. You will find it works well with many stories, and listeners can immediately join in on the repetitive words or phrases, making the storytelling more exciting for everyone.

Having mastered a few signs, children will develop an appreciation and understanding of sign language, and its role as a commonly used language throughout the world. Millions of people with a hearing loss use sign language because it's a very effective way of communicating. Today a hearing loss does not prevent people from achieving their goals.

Why combine sign language and storytelling?

Telling a story while signing a few of the key words is a great way to completely capture your listeners' interest. Once you learn some basic signs, you'll be amazed how often these words appear in other stories. Children will be eager to participate in the storytelling by joining you in signing repetitive phrases.

Try having individual volunteers each sign a particular word from the story. The phases and words are repeated so often, that by the end of the story, everyone knows each sign as well as the refrain.

Besides being beautiful and entertaining, signs are a helpful memory jogger when children retell stories to parents and siblings. Before you know it, parents will be involved, looking forward to hearing the sign language stories their children learn at school. They can even help their child create new stories with the signs they learn!

Do you need to have special training in sign language or be a seasoned storyteller?

No! These signs and stories are designed to be used by everyone. They are simple and easy to do. You may use as many or as few signs as you wish to tell your story. The stories are not dependent on the signs. All you have to do is read the story and practice the signs a few times.

This book's intent is to use signs to enrich the storytelling experience. Because the signs are used in isolation, in some cases, they do not reflect the linguistic rules of sign language.

How do you get started telling sign language stories?

1. Choose your story and read it over several times. Practice the signs that go with the story.

2. During your telling of the story, sign words only as often and as quickly as you feel comfortable. Trying to sign all the words repeatedly the first time you tell the story can be difficult. The signing should not slow the story down or affect your delivery. Signing a greater number of words will become easier after you tell several stories. You will be surprised at how quickly you pick this up.

   For purposes of clarity, all of the words that have signs appear in boldface type throughout the story. You will want to choose how often you do a particular sign.

3. Decide how you want your listeners to be involved. The story that you select helps determine the way you involve the listeners. Here are several possibilities:

   - Children can listen to you and watch you do the signs as the story unfolds.

   - All the listeners can do the repetitive phrase with you.

   - Individuals or groups of children can "be in charge" of a word, and sign their word each time it is mentioned in the story.

4. While you are telling the story, you may wish to have this book open on your lap. This makes it very easy to refer back to the signs or story at any time.

5. Retell the story at least once. Retelling the story gives the listener a second chance to enjoy it as well as to learn the story and the signs. Stories can and should be changed by each storyteller, and a story will be a little bit different each time it is told.

6. Send home copies of the parent letter (p. 71) and story signs. Parents will appreciate that you are taking the time to communicate with them, and students will enjoy sharing the signs with their families. Adding your own letterhead or clip art will personalize your letter.

How can you and your students create original sign language stories?

1. Decide on a story or poem to tell, then choose several words to sign that are an integral part of the story or poem. Or first choose several favorite words to sign. Then find or write a story involving those signs.

2. Practice telling the story and signing the words you have chosen.

3. Teach students the story elements. Every story needs the following:

   a. an introduction

   b. characters

   c. location or setting

   d. action or plot

   e. resolution or good ending

4. Have children work in groups or on their own. Many skills are involved in selecting a story, deciding which signs to use and preparing for presentation.

This is a great way to encourage children who are experiencing difficulty in reading. Make a wide selection of picture books available for students. Books that have a repetitive phrase or lots of animals work well. Encourage children to read several before selecting a story to use as the basis for their own telling. This allows older students to enjoy books they might otherwise overlook.

Expect a wide range of stories from your listeners. Their stories might be similar to one that you have just told. That is great —and quite a compliment to you.

5. After practicing several times, your storytellers will be ready to present their story to the rest of the group. After their presentation, you might want to reward each child with a "Storyteller's Certificate" or another story told by you.

Dear Parents,

Your child is becoming a storyteller and learning sign language at the same time! We have enjoyed telling the attached story several times together as a class.

Storytelling is very important for your child. Children learn so much when they are involved in listening to a story. They also learn a lot when they retell the story to you. They learn the sequence of the story (what happens first, second, last). They learn the difference between reality and fantasy. Their memory improves. Most importantly, they become more confident and creative!

Sign language is as beautiful as a ballet! Learning signs helps children increase their awareness and appreciation of all physically challenged people.

Please take a minute to enjoy this story with your child. You'll be amazed at what a good storyteller your child has become!

Sincerely,

Sign Language Alphabet

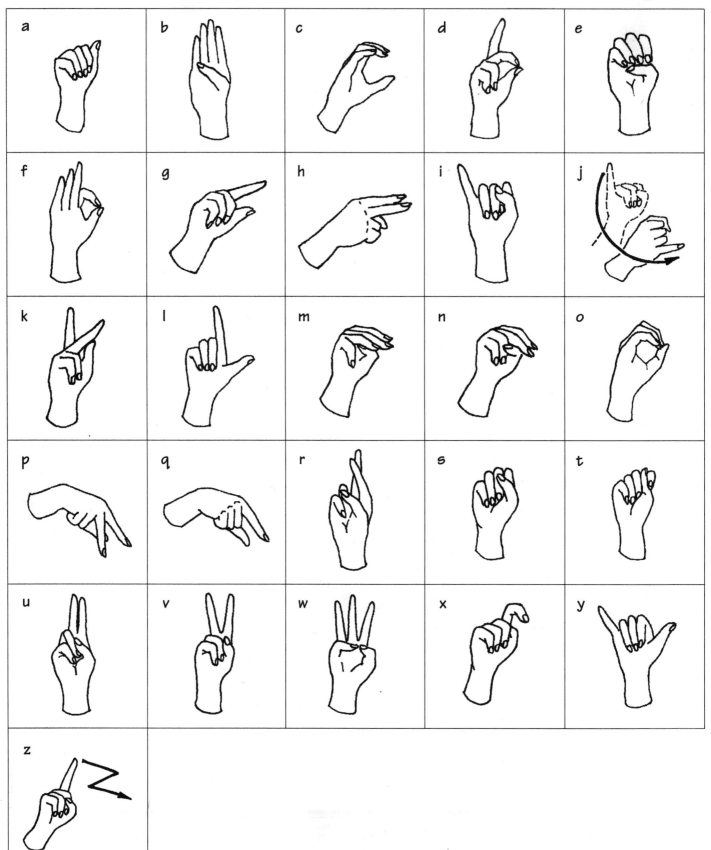

Sign Language Numbers

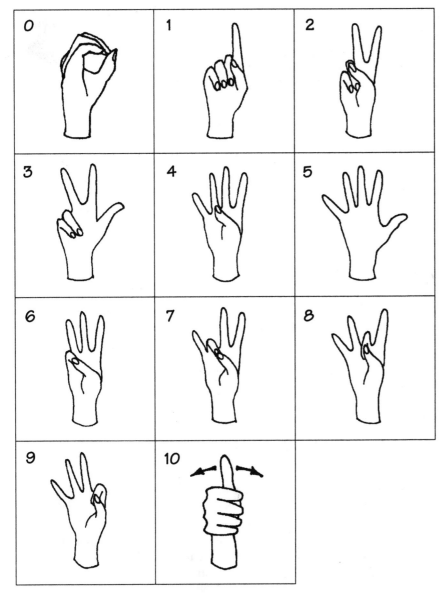

Storyknifing Directions

Storyknifing is an intriguing name that is based in history. In the late nineteenth century, anthropologists and ethnologists discovered that the Inuit people told stories to each other while drawing pictures in the winter snow and summer mud. To draw their pictures they used a rounded knife made of whalebone. Their method of storytelling came to be known as storyknifing.

As you tell these stories you will be drawing a picture. Today you can use markers, chalk, or crayons! At the end of the story, you will also have completed a drawing to share with your listeners.

Why combine storytelling and storyknifing?

Telling a story while drawing a picture is a great way to completely capture your listeners' interest. This is an unusual approach to storytelling and a memorable one based in centuries of tradition. Most children love to draw and spend lots of time at it. After listening to a storyknifing story, children will often take their own drawings and turn them into a story.

Do you need to be an artist or seasoned storyteller?

No! All you need to do is trace! The pictures are designed to be used with any size paper.

How do you get started telling storyknifing stories?

1. First place a piece of paper over the picture in this book. Trace all lines lightly with a pencil. Note where you will place the tape.

2. The drawing steps are loosely related to the story. As the character goes places or does something, you add a new line to your picture.

3. Practice telling your story while drawing so that it becomes natural to talk and draw at the same time. Becoming familiar with the story and the drawing allows you to present the story easily and develop a natural rapport with your listeners.

    If you forget what comes next or get stuck in a story, ask the listeners to repeat what's happened thus far (giving you time to think) or suggest what could come next.

    Do not tell the class what object you are drawing. After hearing a few stories, children will begin guessing about the object you're drawing before you're finished. You'll be able to tell by a child's facial expression when he or she has identified the picture. If you notice a listener just bursting

to "spill" the answer, recognize him or her quietly with an aside such as "Shhh...it's a secret."

4. When you're storytelling to a large group, you'll want to tape the drawing paper to a wall. You can also use a chalkboard, overhead projector or dry eraser board. You can enlarge the picture if working with a larger group. If you have just a few listeners, everyone can sit around a table.

5. Retell the story at least once. Retelling the story gives the listener a second chance to enjoy it as well as to learn the story and the drawing steps. Stories can and should be changed by each storyteller, and a story will be a little different each time it is told.

How can you create your own storyknifing stories?

1. Decide on a story to tell. Then choose something to draw that is an integral part of the story. Or, choose an object to draw, then find or write a story involving that object. "How to Draw" books are available in most libraries and are a great resource for ideas.

2. During the telling, relate the drawing steps to the storyline. For example, as a character goes places or does things, add new lines to your picture.

3. This is a great time to teach the story elements. Every story needs the following: an introduction, characters, location or setting, action or plot, and resolution of plot

4. If you feel the picture will be easily guessed while you are telling the story, draw your picture upside down or sideways.

5. Expect simple, imperfect drawings and stories from your students. Their stories might even be remarkably similar to one you have told. This is fine, and quite a compliment to you.

6. Plan to have several sheets of paper for each student. Encourage them to tell their story to themselves first and then to a friend. Students may prefer to work together in writing and telling their story. When they tell their story to you, you can help them refine it.

7. After several practices with small groups of friends, your storytellers will be ready to present to the rest of the class. After their presentation, you might want to present each child with a "Storyteller's Certificate" or another story told by you.

Story Puzzles Directions

What Are Story Puzzles?

Story Puzzles are a variation of tangrams. Tangrams are wonderful ancient Chinese puzzles that are still used today by children and adults. Each tangram consists of a square which is cut into seven pieces. (Tan means piece.) Pictures can be created with these pieces. All seven pieces must be used. They must touch but no pieces may overlap.

I really liked these puzzles and wanted to involve children in using them to tell their own stories. However, my students and I discovered that the requirement to use all seven pieces was difficult for us. Also, we wanted pieces with curves so that we could make pictures of a flower, or the sun in a less abstract manner. I added three pieces on each end of the tangram puzzles which gave us a total of thirteen pieces.

Why combine storytelling and story puzzles?

Telling a story while making pictures with puzzle pieces is fun! It is also a great way to completely capture your listeners' interest. This is an unusual approach to storytelling and a memorable one based in tradition. Your story will have lots of action because you move the pieces around to make different pictures. Most children love to work with puzzles and spend lots of time at this. After hearing your puzzle story, your listeners will want their own copy of the puzzle pieces so that they can tell their own stories.

Do you need to be an artist or seasoned storyteller?

No! All you need to do is to make a copy of the puzzle page in this book and to cut the pieces out. The puzzle pieces will enhance any story you tell. You arrange your pieces in any way you wish during your story.

How do you get started telling story puzzle stories?

1. Become familiar with the story you want to tell. Copy and cut out the puzzle pieces. There are two sizes so that you can choose the size that works the best for you.

2. Practice moving the pieces around so that you can easily make the figures suggested in the diagrams. Keep the book open to the story and diagrams so that you may refer to them quickly and easily.

3. If you are telling to a small group, you can all sit in a circle. Tell your story as you move the puzzle pieces around on a large piece of poster board or construction paper. Choose the color of the background paper to coordinate with your story.

To further enhance your story, you may color or draw on the back of your pieces. For example, color the two large triangles to make butterfly wings. You may cover the pieces with construction paper, tape them together, or fold them to give a three-dimensional look. If you are telling to a larger group, you may wish to use the overhead projector.

4. Retell the story at least once. Retelling the story gives the listeners a second chance to enjoy it as well as to learn the story and the story puzzle figures. Stories can and should be changed by each storyteller, and a story will be a little different each time it is told.

5. In this book, the pieces have been shaded or coded to indicate the type of action you will take with each piece in the step-by-step illustrations. This makes it easy to see which pieces to add or remove as you tell the story.

   Use the following as a guide for actions in the stories Black: piece to add Gray: pieces to be removed Outlined: pieces that remain in picture Arrows: pieces to be moved or that indicate action

How can you integrate story puzzles into the curriculum?

Language Arts: This is a great time to teach the story elements. Every story needs the following: an introduction, characters, location or setting, action or plot, and resolution or a good ending.

After students decide on a story that they would like to write or tell, use their stories to teach the actual writing process. My students are always amazed at the many steps involved in the writing process.

Brainstorming, or writing down lots of ideas is a good place to start. Then students could make a story map or web. Outlining the plot, writing a paragraph to describe their main character, writing several different endings to their story, using first person or third person narrative are all possibilities to get students involved in writing. Students could also compare and contrast their story to other stories.

Science and history: Use the story puzzle pieces to represent objects or ideas in science and history. You could make a kite when telling the story of Benjamin Franklin's famous experiment during a thunderstorm. A microscope made from the puzzle pieces will spark students' interest in several different concepts you introduce. A ship or canoe graphically demonstrates a story about explorers and their adventures. A simple house might represent the building where the signing of an historic document took place.

Math: If you are teaching a geometry unit, you will want to involve you students in learning to identify a parallelogram, triangle, square, and polygon. You could ask them to draw these shapes, and then identify them using the puzzle pieces.

Challenge them to make objects with their pieces. Which pieces are symmetrical? Where is the line of symmetry? Can you put several pieces together to make a different, yet symmetrical shape?

You and your students will be making objects that are representational. But also have fun constructing more abstract objects that come right out of your imagination! Tell your listeners about your abstract object as your story unfolds.

In many stories, you will need a majority of the pieces to construct your next picture. Remove the current picture before beginning your new picture. You could also work with two or more sets if you wish to create several pictures.

How can you and your listeners start creating your own story puzzles?

1. Give each student a copy of either size of the puzzle pieces. Have them cut the pieces apart. (I give each child an envelope for storing their puzzle pieces.)

2. Let the students play with the shapes. Encourage them to use their imagination and be open-minded. They should not let preconceived notions hamper their creativity. Many times students will get story ideas from the figures they create with their pieces. One student explained to me that he wanted to write a story about a fox because "that's what the triangles kept making themselves into."

3. Students may write their own stories or tell a story that they are already familiar with. Students should create figures and objects related to their story. Figures may be as abstract as desired.

4. As their character goes places or does things, students can add or remove pieces. More permanent figures may be made by taping the pieces together and then coloring them.

It is really fun to show action with the pieces. For example, lightning (piece F) can strike a tree (pieces C, G, D) and the tree can break apart (scatter pieces around). Students can actually fly their spaceship across their paper, flipping down the wings enroute. A child can make a flower wilt by moving the pieces down a bit.

Show a day from sunrise to sunset by moving the sun (circle of A pieces) across the page. Make a face and show sadness by using your fingers to trace the path of tears down the face.

In summary, you may show action by sliding, folding, coloring, taping, ripping, wadding up, blowing or covering up the puzzle pieces.

5. Use either the black or the white side of the pieces. I had always used the black side when telling these stories, but when my students started creating their own stories with their puzzle sets, the first thing they did was color and draw on the pieces. They created pictures using what I had thought of as the back of the pieces!

6. It is easy to copy extra sets of puzzle pieces. If your students color a set for one particular story, they will need a new set for their next story. Sometimes students will use more than one complete set for their story. You may give your students as many copies of puzzle pieces as they need for their different stories!

7. Expect a wide range of figures and stories from your students. Their stories might even be remarkably similar to one you have told. That's great and quite a compliment to you.

8. Students may wish to work with a partner. One person tells the story and the other person moves the pieces around. Many times they will switch positions halfway through their story.

9. Encourage students to tell their story to themselves first and then to a friend. They may want to put their story in writing, make a story web, or outline. When they tell their story to you, you can help them refine it.

10. You may wish to create more permanent puzzle pieces cut from cardboard or foam core. Puzzle pieces can be used on flannelboards or metal dry marker boards with applied backings of flannel/Velcro or magnetic tape, respectively.

11. After several practices with small groups of friends, your storytellers will be ready to present to the rest of the class. After their presentation, you might want to give each child a "Storyteller's Certificate" or tell another story yourself.